IRON

ED'

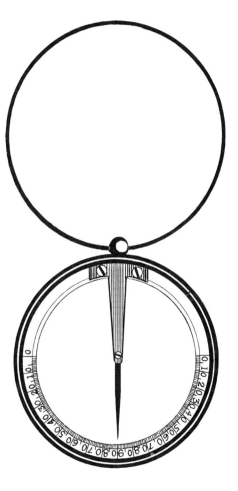

Thomas P. Fitzpatrick, Illustrator

IRON MINE TRAILS

By Edward J. Lenik

First Edition, 1996
Reprinted with revisions, 1999

NEW YORK-NEW JERSEY TRAIL CONFERENCE 1920

Book Design by: **Glenn Scherer, Word & Image**
Cover Design by: **Steve Butfilowski**
Illustrations by: **Thomas Fitzpatrick**
Edited by: **Daniel D. Chazin** and **Nancy L. Gibbs**

Copyright © 1996
Arkaeoloji Ink, Butler, New Jersey.

Published by
New York-New Jersey Trail Conference
    G.P.O. Box 2250
    New York, New York 10016

Library of Congress Cataloging-in-Publication Data

Lenik, Edward J.
    Iron mine trails / by Edward J. Lenik. — 1st ed.
        p.   cm.
    Includes bibliographical references and index.
    ISBN 1-880775-07-7
    1. Hudson Highlands (N.Y.)—Guidebooks. 2. New
Jersey Highlands (N.J.)—Guidebooks. 3. Hiking—New York
(State)—Hudson Highlands--Guidebooks. 4. Hiking—New
Jersey—New Jersey Highlands—Guidebooks. 5. Iron mines
and mining—New York (State)—Hudson Highlands—
Guidebooks. 6. Iron mines and mining—New Jersey—New
Jersey Highlands—Guidebooks. I. Title.
F127.HBL46 1996
917.47'30443—dc20   96-30423
                                     CIP

FOR MY SONS ED, DOUG, FRANK, AND DAN
WHO OFTEN ASKED ME
"WHY DO WE ALWAYS HIKE UPHILL?"

I've been a-hitting some hard-rock mining,
*   I thought you know'd-*
I've been a-leaning on a pressure drill
*   way down the road.*
Hammer flying, air hose sucking
Six foot of mud and I sure been a-mucking
And I been a-having some hard travellin', Lord.

I've been a-working at the foundry,
*   I thought you know'd-*
I've been a-pouring red-hot slag
*   way down the road.*
I've been blasting, I've been firing
And I've been pouring red-hot iron
And I've been a-having some hard travellin', Lord.

— WOODY GUTHRIE
"Hard Travellin'"
(folk song, c. 1939)

The New York-New Jersey Trail Conference

The New York-New Jersey Trail Conference is a nonprofit federation of nearly 10,000 individuals and 85 hiking and environmental organizations working to build and maintain foot trails and to preserve open space.

The Conference was formed in 1920, and its founders built the first section of the Appalachian Trail in 1923. Today, our hiking trail network includes 1,300 miles of marked trails, extending from the Catskills and Taconics south to the Delaware Water Gap. The Conference is supported by membership dues, publication sales and donations – along with thousands of hours of volunteer time. Members receive the bimonthly *Trail Walker*, can purchase our maps and guides at a 20-25% discount, use the extensive Conference library, get substantial discounts at over 20 outdoor stores and trailside lodges… and more.

Current dues start at just $18 (12.50 for students, seniors and those with limited income; $23 for a family). For more information, write to us at 232 Madison Avenue, New York, NY 10016, or call (212) 685-9699. You can also contact us via e-mail at nynjtc@aol.com or visit our Web site at: http://acheron.watson.ibm.com/~trails

Contents

Illustrations

Figure 1: Entrance to Hibernia Mine.
(Harper's New Monthly Magazine, 1860.)

Preface

> Man puts his hand to the flinty rock
> And overturns mountains by the roots.
> He cuts out channels in the rocks,
> And his eye sees every precious thing.
> He binds up the streams so that they do not trickle,
> And the thing that is hid, he brings forth to light.
>
> — *Job 28:9-11.*

*W*e hike the New York-New Jersey Highlands every free day we can, rounding up whichever friends and relations we can get up on their feet, or setting off by ourselves. We are archaeologists: students of antiquity. We usually have an old road to follow or a mine to find, a notation on an old map, an obscure item from an old history book. Ours are not nature hikes, although we rarely miss noting the presence of animals, animal tracks, familiar and unusual plants, or geological wonders. We do not avoid scenic lookouts; we enjoy them with a sense of sharing an experience with people who have been here before us.

People. Our perceptions always come back to the human use of a landscape, and our curiosity is engaged by the traces of human activities we find. Who was here before us? What was their business here? How did they change the landscape? We read the woods and swamps and mountains and trails for the imprint of human industry much as a scholar reads his books. We follow old roads, now choked with trees and brush, to learn where they came from and where they were going. We watch the ground the way birders watch the sky.

This is a field guide for historical hikers. It is meant to be used with the maps produced by the New York-New Jersey Trail Conference. In most instances, trail names, blazes and access are based on these maps. We have not given you trail time for each mine, because we expect you to take your own time getting there and take a while to look around when you do. You might want to remember that many of the mines are *up* some mountains, and going *up* takes longer than it looks like it should on the maps.

New York and New Jersey have preserved vast portions of the Highlands. We know them today as tranquil nature reserves providing respite from the urban industrial cacophony of our everyday worlds. Read this book and remember that, in days past, these mountains reverberated with the noise and upheaval of labor-intensive industries. Stand in the silent woods and hear the roar of the past.

True to our archaeological calling, we have located, measured and described the features you will find at each of these mine sites. We have not excavated them. They are nonrenewable cultural resources, and we respect their integrity. We expect you will do the same. You do not pick the flowers, you do not pick the artifacts, and you do not pothunt archaeological sites. Explore and enjoy the evidence of past human activity, but make your passing this way as undetectable as possible.

NANCY L. GIBBS
Editor, *Arkaeoloji Ink*
Butler, New Jersey

Figure 2:
Iron mine trail friends at the Bradley Mine, Harriman State Park, NY.

A Brief History of Iron Mining in the Highlands

*T*he rugged and forested Highlands physiographic province of northern New Jersey and southeastern New York contains an abundant quantity of rich iron ore which lies deeply buried below the surface of the ground. These iron deposits are mostly magnetite, a black, hard rock ore which is magnetic (hence the name). Some brown hematite is present as well. The discovery of the Highlands iron ore deposits, together with the presence of a vast virgin forest which could be cut to provide charcoal fuel, and fast-flowing rivers and streams to provide waterpower, led to the establishment of iron manufacturing in the region.

The first European explorers in the 17th century came in search of mineral wealth such as gold and silver, but these noble metals were not to be found, or were found only in minute traces. Disappointed, the explorers quickly discovered other opportunities to exploit the natural resources of the area, such as timber and furs. Settlers and farmers followed, approaching and penetrating the rugged Highlands region by the early 18th century.

Cornelius Board discovered the first iron ore deposits in the northern Highlands region in the 1730s. By the early 1740s, he had established forges at Ringwood, New Jersey, and at Sterling Lake, New York. Shortly thereafter, the Ogden family of Newark acquired extensive tracts of land from Board and the Proprietors of East Jersey in order to further exploit and develop the iron resources of the region.

These early iron entrepreneurs were aided in their search for ore deposits by the local Indian bands. The Indians showed the European prospectors the many outcrops of black

**Figure 3: Examining the interior of a mine.
(Harper's New Monthly Magazine, 1860.)**

rock, which they quickly recognized as magnetite iron ore.
Between 1735 and 1749, Charles Clinton surveyed a major
portion of the Hudson Highlands, and often recorded the
character and value of the land. In his survey of the
Cheesecocks Patent, Clinton wrote in his field notes that "iron
ore was discovered by the Indians and appears plentiful
there," referring to a lot near present-day Mombasha Lake in
Orange County, New York. Many of the peaks in the Highlands
region bear witness to these early discoveries by their topographic names, such as Black Mountain or Black Rock.

From the middle of the 18th century to the end of the 19th
century, numerous furnaces, forges and iron mines were
established in the Highlands region. Prospecting for ore —
using compass and dip needle to discover underground veins
— continued throughout this period. Iron deposits in the
Highlands were magnetic and were thus detected by magnetic
surveys. By tracing lines of magnetic attraction on the surface
using compass and dip needle, the positions of bands of ore-

bearing rocks beneath the ground were located and mapped. Many iron deposits were found, mines were opened, and tons of ore were extracted from below the ground.

Some of the mines were successful and produced abundant quantities of good ore — and profits for owners — while others were failures due to impurities in the ore which made smelting difficult or costly, or were simply small veins or deposits impractical to mine. Some of the iron prospecting resulted in the excavation of shallow exploratory pits which were abandoned when little ore was found. During this period, the pits and shafts were worked by miners who removed the ore from the surrounding rock with hand drills, sledge hammers, and black powder explosives. Later, in the 19th century, dynamite was used. The chunks of ore were loaded on wooden or metal cars set on rails and raised out of the mine to the surface.

The hills and valleys of the Highlands region contain many abandoned iron mines and exploratory pits. These sites, once scenes of literally earth-shattering activity, are now quiet, with the shafts often filled with water and rock debris. The open holes and piles of iron ore tailings bear mute testimony to this once-active industry, and await rediscovery by curious historical hikers.

This book presents a brief history of many of the iron mines in the northern Highlands, together with generalized maps of the areas in which they are found. Inquisitive hikers can visit these sites and imagine the intense activity that once took place: the rock drilling, blasting, digging, crushing and hauling of ore. It was difficult and often dangerous work.

> **Those visiting the iron mine sites are cautioned not to enter the shafts or pits. These areas can be dangerous and should not be explored alone.**

Figure 4: Interior of Hibernia Mine.
(Harper's New Monthly Magazine, 1860.)

The Technology of Mining

*B*etween 1740 and the early years of the 20th century, numerous iron mines were opened in the Highlands region. Prospecting for iron ore was particularly extensive during the last quarter of the 19th century, and was stimulated by the tremendous growth and development of our nation. Nearly every Highlands farm which indicated some level of magnetic attraction was explored and tested for the presence of profitable ore veins.

In general, the iron ore deposits in the Highlands consist of a series of parallel belts that trend in a northeasterly to southwesterly direction. Ore deposits are not continuous. Each belt contains a series of deposits that have the same general direction and inclination. The ore beds are usually long and narrow strips with limited exposure at the surface, and plunge toward the northeast. The surface outcrops of ore occur on or near the top of a mountain or ridge and at the southwestern end of the deposit.

Magnetite iron ore is highly magnetic; thus, a magnetic needle or surveyor's compass was used for exploration and detection. However, a compass does not indicate the quantity and extent of an ore deposit. The method employed in exploring for ore was as follows:

The compass was held level in a person's hand, thus allowing the needle to swing freely. The ore prospector then walked in a northwesterly or southeasterly direction at right angles to the direction of the deposit. If iron ore was present, the magnetic pole of the deposit which was nearest would begin to attract the opposite pole of the needle. This attraction would grow stronger until the prospector reached a point directly over the deposit. At this position, the compass needle settled firmly in the direction of the long axis of the ore deposit. The prospector then plotted on paper the position of the ore deposit including its strike, dip, surface and intermittent nature.

Once an ore deposit was located, its extent and quality would be determined by the excavation of small test pits. If the quality of the ore was considered to be good and the quantity present sufficient, a mine was opened and worked on a larger scale. This exploratory procedure was extremely important because in the Highlands region the quantity of ore was small in proportion to the total material extracted. In fact, even a good mine produced more rock than ore.

When iron ore was found in large quantities near the surface, it was mined in open pits or trenches. The surface rock and soils were removed first, and the deposit was worked in a series of levels or terraces. The side walls of pits and trenches were sloped inward or braced with timbers to prevent the rock from crumbling and collapsing. Drainage ditches were dug to remove the water from the work area.

The early excavation methods and tools used in underground mining were simple and essential low-tech in nature.

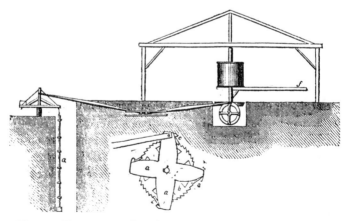

Figure 5: Horse-powered machine used for pumping and hoisting.
(Second Annual Report of the Geological Survey
of the State of New Jersey, 1855.)

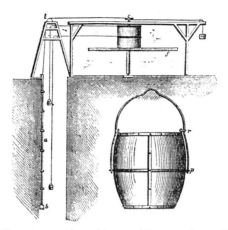

Figure 6: Horse-powered machine used for pumping and hoisting.
(Second Annual Report of the Geological Survey
of the State of New Jersey, 1855.)

They included black powder for blasting, and picks and shovels for "mucking out" the loosened ore. Drilling into the ore body was done in one of two ways: one miner using a short hammer and a short, hardened steel drill, or two miners with one holding a long drill and the other driving with a long hammer. A day's work was measured in drill lengths, with drilling beginning at the start of the day shift and ending when the hole was ready for charging. After the hole was drilled, a charge of black powder was packed into it along with a slow-match fuse. One of the great terrors of a miner's life was a black powder charge that didn't go off, requiring him to go back "in the hole" to fix the problem and hope the blast wasn't just late. This method persisted until the 1870s.

In 1867 dynamite was invented, and in 1869 the mechanical drill run by compressed air was invented. These two inventions created a technological revolution in the mining industry. Dynamite was safer and easier to control than black powder. A steam engine-driven air compressor for the mechanical drill was generally installed outside the mine, and air lines were extended to the drills under ground. Most mines were worked on a small scale, with only a few miners and support personnel.

Underground mining of iron ore required a hoisting mechanism to get miners, waste rock, ore and equipment in and out of the mine. Again, the simplest low-tech method was human or animal power. Examples include hand carrying of ore and waste rock up a ladder, or the use of a windlass — a hand-operated winch — to raise and lower a container. In some mines, wooden or metal cars set on narrow-gauge iron rails were raised to the surface by animal and human power. Later, small steam engines were used to pull ore cars up an inclined ramp.

The most common hoisting system utilized in the 19th and early 20th centuries was the head frame — a derrick-like structure erected over a mine shaft. There was a drum or sheave at the top of the head frame over which passed a rope, cable or chain. An engine pulled the cable to raise and lower an iron frame cage which contained miners, ore or equipment. Breakage of the iron rope or chain was always a deadly hazard. Stronger steel cable was not available for use until after 1840.

Miners encountered many difficulties and dangers, the most formidable of which were problems of ventilation and drainage. Ventilation in the mines was generally poor and dangerous to the miners' health. In the 19th century, miners frequently carried canaries in cages into the mines to serve as an early warning system of foul air. If the bird died suddenly, miners had to get out immediately. The early methods employed in providing fresh air included simple draft ventilation, that is, using shafts and adits to siphon air in and out of a mine. Another technique used was forcing air into the mine by means of bellows.

The flooding of mines and constant water seepage was a common and continuing problem. Miners often stood knee-deep in water. Early mines were bailed out using buckets lifted by windlasses; later, steam engine pumps were used. The first steam engine in America was built in 1755 to dewater the Schuyler Copper Mines in North Arlington, New Jersey.

Finally, after the ore was mined, mechanical crushing and grinding methods (*e.g.*, stamping mills) were employed to reduce the size of the ore and to remove waste rock. Workers stood and picked rock out of the stream of crushed ore passing them on a moving conveyor belt. The ore was also roasted and heated to drive off impurities such as sulphur. These operations were generally performed near the site of the smelter or blast furnace rather than at the mines themselves. In the late 19th and early 20th centuries, large mining complexes such as those at Ringwood and Sterling had facilities for these operations nearby.

Figure 7: Dickerson Mine, circa 1855.
(Second Annual Report of the Geological Survey
of the State of New Jersey, 1856.)

Figure 8: Gallery in Byram Mine.
(Harper's New Monthly Magazine, 1860.)

Highland Miners' Folklore

A miner's workday consisted of exposure to bad air, inhaling rock dust, standing in water, and a constant fear of explosion, cave-in or suffocation. One can easily picture these mining conditions: the darkness, the cramped spaces, the hard drilling, the dim torches using up what precious oxygen there was. Charles Green, a miner at the O'Neill Mines in the 1870s, recalled "a glance down a long black tunnel at different groups with their glowing candles gave the effect of lightning bugs." This occupational environment led to the development of miner's folklore and myths.

The presence of rats in the mines was tolerated and respected in the belief that these creatures could predict disaster. Candle stubs were left for the rats to eat. When the mine rats began leaving and scurrying for the surface, this was a sure signal for the men to leave quickly while they still had time. "For two days the rats were coming out of Old Number Four, and everyone knew what that meant. The big gray fellows were determined to reach the surface and would have fought a man on the ladders. Rats knew when a cave-in was coming, long before the men suspected it, and on the second night Old Number Four let loose sure enough. No one was in it thanks to the rats, and no one has been very far in it since," related Charles Green.

A number of different events were thought to bring bad luck to the miners. For example, whistling in the mines was considered bad luck, as was the number thirteen. In fact, mines were usually closed on Friday the 13th. Also, it was bad luck for a woman to enter a mine, and men would leave the diggings if they saw a woman there.

Several mines, particularly those that were shut down, were said to be inhabited by ghosts. Such stories are often told about the Ringwood group of mines. One such tale relates to the Peter's Mine, which was a major source of iron ore for over 200 years. During its years of production activity, miners often spoke of the presence of a ghost within its deep shafts and corridors. Miners reported hearing the ghost knocking on the walls and said that it was lonely and wanted company. The sound of the ghost knocking was often followed by an accident.

Figure 9: A miner.
(Harper's New Monthly Magazine, 1860.)

Highland Miners' Lives

*T*hose of us who have not "been very far in it ever since" wonder about the lives of those who lived and worked in these Highland mines. At some of the sites, one will find traces of dwellings; others are close enough to settlements to have provided seasonal work for part-time local labor.

In 1938, C. Boehm Rosa interviewed Charles Green, then 76 years old, who had gone to work at the O'Neill Mines near Monroe, New York, at the age of nine in 1871. First, Green drove mules around the winch that hauled ore out of the mine. Sometimes he hauled water and fetched drills. At the age of twelve, he became a regular miner on a seven-and-a-half-foot drill, swinging a nine-pound hammer. "The drills, all operated by hammer and brawn, were of three sizes. Each had its special purpose. There was the stoop or seven-and-a-half-foot drill, driven into the rock wall a couple of feet off the floor. Next, came the breast or five-foot drill, to be sunk midway up the wall. Third, the head or three-foot drill, driven in at a level with the head. When the holes were touched off with explosives, they broke off the ore in a scoop-like section."

Green earned eighty-one cents a day, on which "I kept a family of five better than I could do it today on much more." Miners at O'Neill lived in a community of about forty frame houses full of families and boarders. They were paid by the month and bought their supplies at the company store at Arden, New York. "The clerk merely deducted the amount of purchases from the payroll, and sometimes a workman had no pay at all by the end of the month. The company was good about that. If a person had 'overdrawn' his pay, but sent an order for food or clothing, he always got his supplies. Company teamsters took the orders and on certain days delivered to certain mines."

**Figure 10: Digging for ore by the method called stoping.
(Harper's New Monthly Magazine, 1860.)**

"It was hell in Monroe on Saturday nights. There were always ten or twelve free-for-all fights in the streets or saloons. One place in particular stands out in my memory. That was a saloon at about the site of W.C. Stevenson's market today at One North Main Street. Several Sunday mornings found this establishment without a door or window left intact. No one was ever arrested. Goshen Jail wouldn't have held them all. Usually some of the men would settle with the proprietor on Sunday and then take a collection at the mines to repair the damage."

Green left mining in 1881 for a career on the Erie Railroad. In his day, the miners were mostly English or Irish, working together for the most part, although he says the Bull Mine was all English. "An Irishman didn't dare show himself at that mine."

Between 1913 and 1917, a sociological survey was made of the families working the Sterling Mines, at the direction of Mrs. E.H. Harriman. Many of the English and Irish families were still there. "He was employed at the Sterling Mine, as was his father before him" is a frequent note in the study files.

Many families still lived in the mine housing and still shopped, now with cash, at the company stores. "The family were living in a tumble-down house on the Hewitt estate, for the man was working at the Hewitt Mine at Ringwood." Some mines had closed, and much of this housing was remote. Social workers found families wary: "They were so shy and suspicious that the children would disappear as if by magic when a stranger approached, and keep perfectly quiet until they were gone; they were like a nest of small partridges."

Some jobs never changed. "He worked alongside his father picking rocks from the conveyor belt." New jobs reflected advances in technology. "Will is employed as an electrician in the mines. Frank runs a machine — a drill — in the mines." The work was still dangerous. "Horace died in a mine accident. Ted was killed by an explosion."

As mining and ironmaking declined, many mining families had members working at other trades. "Edna, who works in a silk mill, earns good wages.... Of her brothers, one is a chauffeur for Mr. Henry Munroe of Tuxedo Park, and one is a butler for Mr. John D. Rockefeller.... The family were employed at the mines, but the high wages at the powder works induced them to go to Haskell [New Jersey]." Others continued the older ways of supplementing the mine wages.

Figure 11: A miner pushing an ore cart.
(Harper's New Monthly Magazine, 1860.)

"Mother braids rugs, pieces quilts and takes in washing. Mary Jane gathers winterberries for the distillery. John, who played the violin, followed the occupations of his father, working at wood chopping jobs, carving wooden spoons and bowls, gathering bark for tanning, and making charcoal."

New immigrants found their way to the mines. "On December 1, 1913, the working population of Sterling Mines consisted of 168 men, of whom forty-two were Native American [of European-American heritage, not Indian, as we now use the term], forty-eight were Slavs, Hungarians and Russians, and seventy-eight were Italians.... Of the forty-eight Slavs, Hungarians, and Russians, seven rent houses and all except one family take in boarders. These people are as a rule comparatively temperate, are exceedingly industrious and thrifty.... The seventy-eight Italian laborers all live in the Italian colony. Six of them are married with families. These live in separate houses, while the seventy-two others live in shanties. The indications are that thrift is practiced to the extent that some of the employees are poorly nourished and consequently inefficient. Several hundred dollars of savings are sent abroad each week."

Many Ramapo Mountain families worked as miners and laborers at the furnaces and forges. Some iron company records exist which reveal the names of local people who were employed and where they lived. Their homes were located in hamlets and villages and were also scattered throughout the mountains. For example, 19th century payroll lists at Ringwood include the names of DeGroat, Defrease, Milligan, Morgan, Suffern and Van Dunk. The Village of Ramapo, another ironmaking community, had inhabitants by the name of Babcock, Call, Conklin, Stalter, Starr, Secor and Youmans; these names are identified with mountain families as well. In the early 20th century, the Sterling group of mines employed members of these families: DeGraw, Dolan, Edwards, Fletcher, Gordon, Jones, McGrady, Osborn, Slawson, Thompson, Van Tassel, Whitehead and Whitmore. Hikers will find remnants of many of these mountain family homesteads throughout the Highlands region.

The O'Neill Mines closed in 1885. Efforts by Bethlehem Steel to expand the Sterling Mines were abandoned in 1923. The Forest of Dean Mines closed on Election Day in 1931. Only the Peter's Mine at Ringwood, N.J., and the mines at Franklin and Dover, N.J., continued to be active into the mid-20th century. Save for these three areas, mining as a livelihood was gone from the Highlands before World War II.

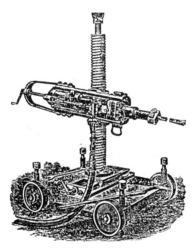

Figure 12: Illustration of Burleigh Mechanical Rock Drill.
(Henry S. Drinker, A Treatise on Explosive Compounds, Machine Rock Drills, and Blasting. John Wiley and Sons, NY, 1883.)

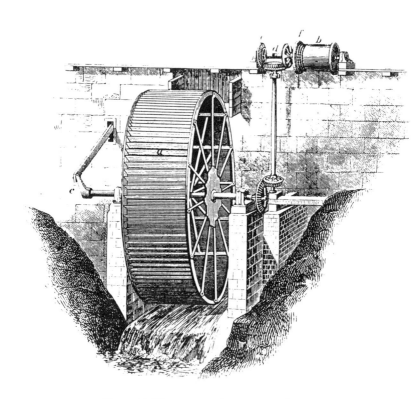

Figure 13: Water-powered pump at Richards Mine.
Second Annual Report of the Geological Survey
of the State of New Jersey, 1855.)

Names of Mines and Ethnicity of Miners

*M*any of the mines in the Highlands region were named after property owners from whom rights to explore for minerals had been procured. Family or personal names attached to mine sites give us a picture of settlement patterns in an area at a particular point in time. Some examples of mines with family names include Whritenour, Patterson, Hewitt, Pierson, Rutherfurd, Cole Farm and Decker in New Jersey, and Hogencamp, Lewis, Christie and Herbert in New York.

Some mines were named after landscape features or geographical locations (Pierson Ridge, Wawayanda, Rockaway Valley, Pine Swamp, Cranberry, Doodletown) or the type of ore found (Blue, Nickel). Some commemorate the people who located them or established industrial enterprises (Roomy, Hasenclever). Others are named after local folklore (Spanish), architectural quality (Surebridge) and function (Pierson Exploration). Finally, the etymology of many mine names remains unknown and the subject of continuing research.

Miners came from a variety of cultural and social backgrounds. They reflect the settlement patterns of various European groups who moved into the region in Colonial and post-Colonial times. The first miners in the New Jersey-New York Highlands were probably of English origin. The first ironmaking activity in the region began at Ringwood, New Jersey around 1740, when Cornelius Board built a forge on the Ringwood River. Shortly thereafter, the Ogden family of Newark acquired extensive tracts of land in the area, built the first blast furnace at Ringwood in 1742, and established the Ringwood Company for the production of iron. The Ringwood Company became one of the largest producers of iron in colonial America.

In 1764, the Ogdens sold their Ringwood Company operations to the American Company, which was organized by a group of London investors headed by Peter Hasenclever, a German. Within a year, Hasenclever brought 535 Germans to New York and New Jersey to work as miners, founders, forgemen, colliers, carpenters, masons and laborers. The total number of immigrants included women and children, so that Hasenclever acted as both colonizer and ironmaster. Under Hasenclever's direction, fifty-three different iron mines were opened in the region.

Local indigenous people, natives of the Ramapo Mountains, also worked in the mines alongside the English and Germans. The 19th century brought new immigrants to the area, in particular the Irish, to work in the iron industry. By the early 20th century, the ethnic mix included Italians and several eastern European groups. The backgrounds of these mining pioneers are often visible on tombstones of long-abandoned cemeteries in the region.

Figure 14: Interior of adit — Sweed's Mine.
(Harper's New Monthly Magazine, 1860.)

Glossary of Cultural Features and Mining Terms

Pits: Defining Their Function

*O*nce you start exploring old mine sites, you will become very aware of pits as you hike and explore other areas. To aid you in understanding these holes, here are some hints about what each pit you encounter was used for:

Borrow Pits: These are often adjacent to old roads, and indicate soil removal. They can be of any shape and do not have tailings or backfill piles nearby.

Charcoal Pits: These woodland features are not actual pits or holes, but flat, circular cleared areas known as "charcoal bottoms." Charcoal is found on or near the surface. The areas may be built up with soil and stonework to create a level platform. Bright green "hearth grass" may cover the surface of these sites.

Charcoal Burners' Huts: These, too, are not pits, although some may appear to be below the surrounding ground level. They are found near charcoal bottoms and consist of a ring or horseshoe pattern of deliberately-laid small boulders outlining the hut floor. The temporary superstructure, often wood and bark, is gone, and only the support stones remain.

Cellar Holes: The remains of a room under a former building. They are square or rectangular in shape, and often well-constructed, usually of cut stone.

Exploratory Pits: Usually shallow holes with tailing or backfill piles nearby. Unlike borrow pits, they can be anywhere on the landscape and are often far from roads. The Highlands region was explored for uranium in the 20th century. Some exploratory pits may be from uranium prospecting, rather than from the earlier periods of iron mining.

Privies: Toilets; also referred to as outhouses or necessaries. They are small, square, or rectangular holes often lined with stone. Some are unlined but have cut stones at the corners to support a wooden superstructure. They are usually found near old buildings or foundations, and often nearly completely filled with earth and rock.

Quarries: Places where rock has been dug or blasted from the earth. Like mines, they have drilled and cut stone in evidence. Broken rock that looks like tailings may also occur, but iron ore will not be present.

Wells: These features are round, of small diameter, and stone-lined. They are deep and water-filled at some level. Like privies, they are part of a complex of buildings or foundations.

Mining Terms and Features

Adit: The horizontal passage or tunnel that is the opening to the mine at the surface.

Concentrate: The ground-up iron-bearing particles after separation from impurities.

Country Rock: The matrix within which the ore body is found.

Cross-Cuts: Horizontal passages running at sharp angles to the long axis of the ore body.

Dip of the Needle / Magnetic Dip: The angle which a magnetic needle, freely suspended, makes with the horizon at a given location.

Drift: An underground horizontal passage or tunnel that follows the vein of the ore.

Drill: An edged or pointed tool that bores holes in rock with its end by revolving or by a succession of blows. A "star" drill, made by die forging and machining, has cutting edges at right angles to one another. A "plug" drill, an older type, made by a blacksmith, has two straight edges which meet to form the point, which is beveled to a cutting edge. The stock for the plug drill was a rod with a square cross-section and chamfered (beveled) corners.

Gangue: Rock containing no ore.

Head Frame: A gallows-like structure, often enclosed, erected over a mine shaft. At the apex of the head frame is a drum or sheave over which a rope or cable passes. Animals, an engine or some other source of power pulled the rope or cable to raise and lower miners, ore and supplies.

Hematite: A non-magnetic oxide of iron represented by the formula Fe_2O_3. It is commonly referred to as red ore because of its color, and because it produces a red streak. The ore contains about seventy percent iron.

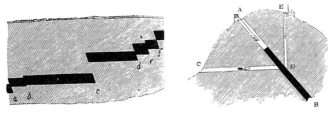

Figures 15 & 16: Vertical cross-section showing ore deposits dislocated by faults (left). Mine cross-section showing vertical, horizontal and inclined shafts. (Harper's New Monthly Magazine, 1860.)

Incline: Descent or downward slope of an ore body. Also refers to an inclined passage excavated at an angle from the vertical.

Lean Ore: Ore with low iron content, or which is lacking in good qualities because it contains sulphur or other impurities.

Limonite: A yellowish-brown hydrous iron oxide commonly called "bog ore." It has an irregular shape and occurs as a soft or earthy mass, or in compact, smooth and dark masses. The most diagnostic feature of limonite is its yellowish-brown streak.

Magnetite: Commonly referred to as black ore. Its chemical formula is Fe_3O_4, and it contains over seventy-two percent iron. The ore is strongly magnetic, hard and heavy, and it produces a black streak.

Mucker: A person who loads mine cars with ore and pushes them through the shafts or tunnels.

Mud Spoon: A crude tool, about twenty inches long, made from brass or copper, and used to clean out rock dust from drilled holes. Some have scribe lines cut into them at one-inch intervals; these were used to measure the depth of the hole to determine the amount of blasting powder needed. This tool was also used to remove the remains of a misfire, and thus was made from brass or copper so as not to cause a spark.

Ore: Any naturally-occurring mineral substance from which metal may be extracted.

Outcrop: Surface exposure of the underlying bedrock through the soil.

Overburden: The overlying earth or rock that covers an ore deposit.

Pillar: A column of rock or ore left in place to support the roof of a mine.

Powder Magazine: A storehouse, usually built into a hillside and covered with earth. Also, a repository for blasting powder or dynamite.

Prospecting: Searching for ore deposits.

Raises: Shafts excavated upward to connect different levels of a mine's interior.

Shaft: A deep vertical or inclined excavation or passage for locating or mining ore.

Shot Ore: An aggregate of small, rounded granular particles of iron, somewhat resembling small shot in size and shape. Also, a type of low-grade or lean ore.

Skip: An iron car that operates on rails; the term also refers to a large hoisting bucket.

Slope: An inclined passage into a mine.

Stope: A horizontal step excavation above or below a level from which ore has been extracted.

Streak: The color of iron ore, which is determined by rubbing a sample on a white unglazed porcelain plate.

Strike: The direction of an inclined bed of ore.

Surface Mining: Open pit mining.

Tailings: Pieces of rock, containing little or no iron, that have been separated from the ore deposit. Also, mine refuse.

Winzes: Shafts sunk downward in the mine's interior.

Figure 17: Head Frame at the Cannon Mine, Ringwood, NJ.

Iron Mines and Trails in New Jersey

Winston Mine

*T*he Winston Mine complex (figure 19) is located along the eastern slope of Monks Mountain in the Borough of Ringwood, Passaic County, New Jersey. The mountain overlooks the Monksville Reservoir and is now a part of Long Pond Ironworks State Park. The hamlet of Monks or Monksville, settled in the early 19th century by pioneering families of that name, is now under the water of the reservoir. This mine complex is easily accessible and can be explored within a few hours. Old roads and hiking trails lead through rock-strewn glens and deep stands of tall timber, contrasting with the open waters of the Monksville Reservoir.

To reach the Winston Mine, park in the boat launch

Figure 18: Pumping out water by steam power. (Second Annual Report of the Geological Survey of the State of New Jersey, 1855.)

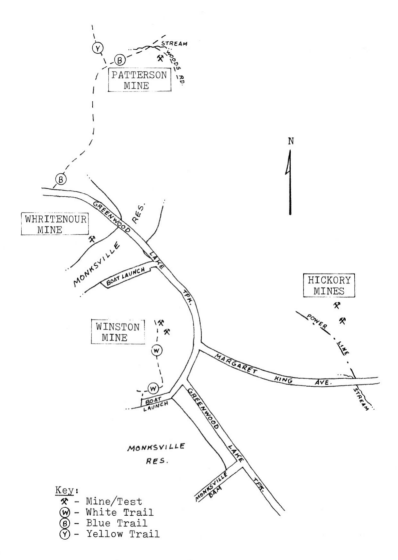

Figure 19: Map showing locations of Winston, Whritenour, Patterson and Hickory Mines.

parking area which is located along the southeastern base of Monks Mountain, just off the Greenwood Lake Turnpike (Passaic County Route 511). To begin the hike, walk to the northwesterly corner of the parking area, and follow a well-defined trail into the woods. You may notice some faded white blazes. Soon you will reach a T-intersection. Turn right, and follow a more clearly blazed trail. This is the white-blazed Monks Trail, which follows the route of an old mining road. Soon the white blazes turn left, leaving the road. The mine complex can be reached by following the Monks Trail or the old road in a northerly direction. However, a hike along the road to the mine is more direct and rewards the mine explorer by providing a clear picture of how difficult it was to haul the ore down the mountain for shipment and processing elsewhere. The old road parallels a beautifully made dry-laid stone fence or wall which extends up the mountain to the right or east of the road. One can easily imagine a pastoral scene with cows grazing to

the east of the stone fence while to the west, wagons and mule teams struggled to bring the ore out.

As you reach the top of the hill, near the end of the stone fence, you will encounter a farm dump including two abandoned automobiles. About 100 feet to the left or west of the road are two small mine openings. The first is an exploratory pit that measures sixteen feet by thirteen feet by five feet in

---

Old roads and hiking trails lead through rock-strewn glens and stands of tall timber

---

depth. A short distance to the north is a second opening that measures fifteen feet by twelve feet and is filled with automobile tires. Adjacent to this opening is a flat level area that once served as a work platform or staging area. This work area measures twenty-nine feet by twenty feet by three feet in height and was carefully constructed, as suggested by an eight-foot section of a stone retaining wall which borders its easterly side. Several small ore piles are present nearby.

Return to the old road and continue hiking in a northerly direction until you come to the junction of the Monks Trail. About 75 feet to the right or east of the road-trail are the principal workings of the Winston Mine complex, including two deep shafts, trenches, and exploratory pits and tailing piles. One vertical shaft measures forty feet in diameter and is about fifty feet deep. Water is present at the bottom of this shaft and a pillar of rock is visible in the entrance at the bottom. A few feet to the southeast is a second deep rectangular pit which measures forty-five feet in length, twenty-five feet in width and twenty-five feet in depth. This shaft also contains water at the bottom.

There are five additional mine openings located in close proximity to the two main shafts. The first is an open trench, fifty feet long, fifteen feet wide and ten feet deep with a narrow entrance on its down-slope or easterly side. Three exploratory pits of varying size and depths are situated to the north and

Figure 20: Miners at Ringwood, NJ, c. 1916 (courtesy of W. Trusewicz)

northeast of the main shafts. Finally, there is one opening, located just to the north of the large vertical shaft, that is fourteen feet by fourteen feet on the surface and eight feet deep; it appears to have served as an air shaft.

Traces of other small exploratory pits are present elsewhere along the slopes of Monks Mountain. A hike along the slopes and summit of the mountain will result in more mine discoveries as well as revealing scenic vistas.

Documentary information regarding the Winston Mines is sparse. Two large mine openings, identified as the "Winston Mines," are shown on a survey map dated 1874-1876. These mines are within a ten-acre mine lot, "No. 5," belonging to Cooper & Hewitt, the proprietors of the nearby Ringwood Mines and Long Pond Ironworks. The survey map also depicts a road beginning at the "West Milford and Pompton Road," now Greenwood Lake Turnpike, and extending to the Winston Mines. However, data regarding its years of operation, the quality of its ore, and the quantity pro-

duced are lacking. The Winston Mine is not identified by this name in the various geological surveys of iron mines which were produced by the State of New Jersey in the late 19th and early 20th centuries.

Iron mines can be pursued in the literature as well as in the field. This is certainly the case with regard to the Winston Mine. Many mines operated intermittently through the years, and ownership (hence their names) changed frequently. It is suggested that the Winston Mine may be the "Monks Mine" which is described in the 1873, 1879, and 1910 geological surveys. The Monks Mine, also known as the Vincent Mine, is described as being located on the north side of the Wanaque River about two miles above Boardville in Pompton Township (now Borough of Ringwood), Passaic County. This description certainly fits the location of the Winston Mine. Historian James M. Ransom states that the Monks Mine was opened shortly after the Civil War and was abandoned by 1890.

Whritenour Mine

*T*he Whritenour Mine (figure 19) is a "farm mine," an exploration that located small veins of ore on land leased from local farmers. The mine is presently situated on the north side of the Monksville Reservoir at a point approximately 900 feet southwest of the Greenwood Lake Turnpike (Passaic County Route 511). To begin your hike to this mine, park in the boat launch parking area located at the northern base of Monks Mountain, opposite Beech Road in the Borough of Ringwood. After parking, walk out to the Greenwood Lake Turnpike, turn left and proceed north-westerly over the causeway that crosses the reservoir. At the end of the causeway, turn left and hike along the northwest shore of the reservoir to the mine site.

The Whritenour Mine consists of a cluster of four pits located near the shore of the reservoir. One pit is situated on elevated ground not far from the water, while two others are located farther up the steep hillside to the west-northwest. The fourth mine pit is located at the shoreline of the reservoir and is completely filled with water. There are several piles of iron ore tailings around each mine hole. There are also cut-and-shaped stone blocks, some with drill marks, scattered throughout the site. The remains of a work-staging area with a stone retaining wall can be

> **The Whritenour Mine consists of a cluster of four pits located near the reservoir shore**

seen on a small flat terrace adjacent to the reservoir. The area of the mine, near the edge of the Monksville Reservoir, is heavily wooded today. At one time, an old road extended from the bank of the Wanaque River up to the mine, but this road is now beneath the water of the reservoir. A fifth mine pit, once visible at the site, is also under water.

The Whritenour Mine was originally worked by a Mr. Henderson and was named the Henderson Mine, but the date of its opening is

Figure 21: Photograph of Dinkey Steam Engine at the Ringwood Mines, c. early 1910s. (Courtesy of North Jersey Highlands Historical Society.)

not known. The Geological Survey of New Jersey for 1881 states that the mine was "reopened" around 1880 by the Greenwood Lake Iron Company. A shaft was sunk to a depth of fifty feet and the underground horizontal passage or drift was forty feet long, following a vein that was four feet wide. The ore was rich and free of sulphur, but contained a great deal of phosphorus. The mine was abandoned after prospecting in the area failed to locate good quantities of ore.

Oral history tells us that there were no buildings or structures at this site and that the mine workers were local people who came to the mines on a daily basis from the homes nearby. To the west of the mine is the abandoned right-of-way of the Montclair and Greenwood Lake Railroad, which passes through a quarried section of bedrock that was known as "Henderson's Cut" — undoubtedly named for the original operator of the mine.

The Ward-Whritenour homestead and farm were located on the south side of the Greenwood Lake Turnpike, on the west side of the Wanaque River. The house was built in 1813 by Henry

Ward. The Ward lands and premises were acquired by Mathias Whritenour in 1833, and the property remained in the Whritenour family well into the 20th century. In 1985, the Whritenour property was acquired by the State of New Jersey for the new Monksville Reservoir. Archaeological data recovery excavations were conducted at the site, and the Whritenour House was relocated to the Long Pond Ironworks.

Patterson Mine

*T*he Patterson Mine (figure 19) is located north-northeast of the Long Pond Ironworks on land formerly known as the Sterling Forest Tract, and recently acquired by Passaic County as parkland. The site lies to the east of the blue-dot-on-white-blazed Sterling Ridge Trail in West Milford, New Jersey.

The route to the Patterson Mine begins on the Greenwood Lake Turnpike (Passaic County Route 511) at the Long Pond Ironworks State Park visitors center (known locally as the "Ye Olde Country Store"). From the visitors center, walk northwesterly, paralleling the Greenwood Lake Turnpike, until you come to an unimproved and gated road on your right. Turn right and enter the Long Pond Ironworks Historic Site. Proceed along this road in a northerly direction, passing the relocated Ward-Ryerson-Patterson House (c. 1780), the Harty House (19th century) and the relocated Whritenour House (c. 1813) on your right. The road crosses a small stream and reaches a nexus of roads within the former ironworks village near the ruin of a general store. Take the road to the right, which is marked with the blue-dot-on-white blazes of the Sterling Ridge Trail, paralleling the Wanaque River on your right until you reach the ruins of the 18th and 19th century blast furnaces.

Pause here and examine the ruins of this once-mighty industrial enterprise which produced cast iron products from iron ore extracted from the nearby mountains. The Long Pond Ironworks was established in 1766 by Peter Hasenclever who was

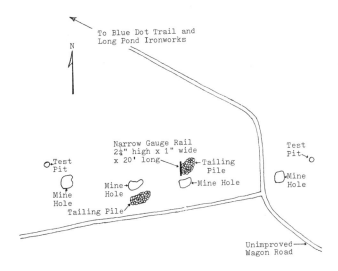

Figure 22: Field sketch of Patterson Mine site.

manager of a business enterprise called the American Company (a.k.a. the London Company) that had purchased and operated the ironworks at Ringwood two years before. Hasenclever's American Company built a blast furnace for smelting iron ore, a forge for producing bar iron, a blacksmith shop, a sawmill, a horse stable, a store, charcoal houses and dwellings for ironworkers at the site. In 1807, Martin Ryerson acquired the Long Pond Ironworks when he pur-chased the Ringwood properties. In 1853, the Long Pond Ironworks together with Ringwood was purchased by Peter Cooper and Abram S. Hewitt. Cooper and Hewitt expanded operations at the site by building two new blast furnaces, an iron ore roaster, and other manufacturing support facilities. Their company, known as the Trenton Iron Company, operated the Long Pond Ironworks until the 1880s, when ironmaking operations at the site ceased forever.

Return to the Sterling Ridge Trail and cross the foot bridge over the Wanaque River. Continue on this trail, which immediately turns left, for about one mile, passing a yellow trail, until you reach an unmarked trail which enters from the right. Take the unmarked trail, and follow it northeasterly up the hillside for about 0.25 mile to the Patterson Mine.

This mine dates from around 1870 and was last worked in 1903. The mine consists of two deep vertical pits, presently filled with water, with large ore piles adjacent to the openings (figure 22). Two additional mine holes and two small exploratory pits are also nearby. In 1988, two sections of narrow-gauge rail were found at one of the mine holes. One of these rail sections is presently curated at the Long Pond Ironworks visitors center. However, no ore was shipped from this mine.

The Patterson Mine is associated with the Ward-Ryerson-Patterson House, which formerly stood on the north side of the Greenwood Lake Turnpike opposite the Whritenour House. The house was built around 1780 and functioned as a farmstead and country inn until 1980. The house and 240 acres of land were purchased in 1842 by George Patterson and remained in the Patterson family for eighty-one years. The property was acquired in 1980 by the State of New Jersey to make way for the new Monksville Reservoir. In 1985, archaeological data recovery excavations were conducted at the site, and the historic Patterson House was moved to the Long Pond Ironworks Historic District.

Hickory Mines

A large exploratory trench and several mine pits are located near the south-central border of the former Sterling Forest tract in the Borough of Ringwood, New Jersey. This 2,000-acre tract of land is now an undeveloped Passaic County Park which has been inappropriately renamed "Tranquility Ridge." This forested tract is situated between the Ringwood Mines area on the east and the Long Pond

Ironworks State Park on the west; in earlier historic times, it was referred to as "unappropriated lands." The mine openings are known as the Hickory Valley Mine and the Hickory Mountain Mine (figure 19).

The Hickory Mines are located on a rugged, wooded and stony hillside to the north of Margaret King Avenue in Ringwood, New Jersey. A small roadside turnoff or parking area is on the north side of Margaret King Avenue, 0.7 mile east of its intersection with the Greenwood Lake Turnpike. The trail begins here; park and begin your hike to the mines by following an old woods road to the north. Almost immediately, the old road crosses a small stream by way of a battered wooden bridge. Cross the stream and follow the old road uphill, passing much trash along the edge of the road, including several abandoned vehicles. Continue for about 750 feet until you reach a fork in the road. Take the road to the right heading uphill and passing underneath the Orange and Rockland Utilities overhead power

lines. Continue on the woods road, which may be flooded in some areas, up the hillside and into the deep woods. After about 800 feet, you will reach a side road which enters the woods road on the left from the northwest. After a short distance, this dirt

These mines are part of the Ringwood group of mines, explored in the late 19th century

road steeply ascends a hill. Here the road is badly eroded, and it has the appearance of a gully. When you reach a plateau or terrace at the top of the climb, the road once again becomes more recognizable as such.

About 300 feet from the junction with the main road, on the left side of the plateau, you will observe the remains of a small horseshoe-shaped structure constructed of boulders and cobbles. This structural ruin is somewhat circular, measures eight feet across and has an entrance which faces northeast. It may be the remains of a charcoal burner's hut or an outbuilding associated with the nearby Hickory Mines. There are several flat areas near the ruin which may be the sites of charcoal bottoms, commonly but erroneously referred to as "pits."

Continue hiking up the road for a short distance to the Hickory Mines site; the workings are situated both to the left and right of the old woods road. On the right is an open water-filled trench, thirty-four feet long, fifteen feet wide and fifteen feet

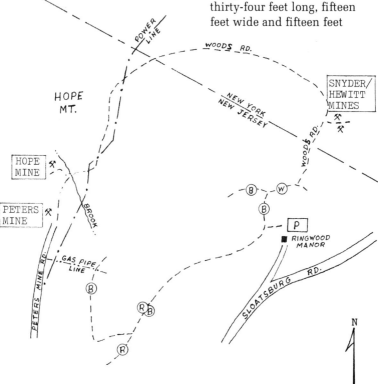

Figure 23: Map showing locations of Snyder, Hewitt, Hope and Peter's Mines.

Key:
⚒ – Mine/Test
ⓦ – White Trail
Ⓑ – Blue Trail
Ⓡ – Red Trail
P – Parking

deep. This mine trench has been cut into the hillside; its open end is on the east and a large tailings pile borders the south side of the trench. A stone retaining wall, constructed of mine rock, extends from the northeast corner of the trench for about thirty feet.

Directly in front of the open end of the trench to the east is a flat terrace of mine rock. There is a rectangular platform on the terrace, constructed of mine tailings, that is twenty-seven feet long, ten feet wide and three to four feet high. This structural feature may have served as a loading platform or as a base for some type of mining equipment.

Return to the old road and explore the area to the west of the mine trench. On the left side of the road, opposite where the road passes through a cut, there is a small circular pit eight feet in diameter, with a pile of tailings at the roadside. Approximately forty feet to the west is a second exploratory pit. This mine opening measures twelve feet by eight feet and is about four feet deep; it is filled with water

and surrounded by tailings.

The Hickory Valley and Hickory Mountain mine openings are prospector's pits and were not worked commercially. They are part of the Ringwood group of mines and were probably explored in the late 19th century.

Snyder and Hewitt Mines

A moderate uphill hike, forty minutes in length, will bring the historical explorer to these two mines (figure 23), which are located within the former Sterling Forest property in Orange County, New York. This property was acquired in February 1998 by the Palisades Interstate Park Commission and now forms a part of Sterling Forest State Park. For information on hiking in this park call (914) 351-5907.

To begin the hike, park in the main lot adjacent to the formal gardens of Ringwood Manor, to the northeast of the Manor. Walk to the northwest corner of the parking lot, and cross a short length of lawn diagonally to a macadam garden path. Turn left and walk west for a short distance until you come to a cross-road. Turn right and walk through the wide entrance in the garden wall, turning left immediately. Proceed west on a gravel estate road, passing the Manor which is on your left, until you come to a road which enters on your right. This junction is the start of the Blue Trail. Turn right and follow an old mine-estate road northward toward the mines. Stay on the mine road — do not follow the Blue Trail, which turns off to the left, or the White Trail, which soon turns off to the right. Continue hiking north along the mine road, which is now unmarked, and pass underneath some overhead electric power lines. A power line maintenance road crosses the mine road here.

A walk of 175 feet north from this point along the mine road will bring you to the New York-New Jersey state line. This boundary is marked by a low rectangular granite stone on the right side of the mine road. The boundary stone is marked with a cross on its top, "NY" on its north side, and "NJ" on its south side. There is a shallow mine pit adjacent to the marker.

The 21st milestone marking the state line is located about 250 feet to the east of the mine road. From the earliest days of European settlement, the bound-

---

The Snyder Mine consists of a large open pit, now water filled, and is about 100 feet in length

---

ary line between the provinces of New York and New Jersey was in dispute. The boundary controversy was not settled until 1769 when a Royal Commission appointed by King George III finally established its position. In 1774, the boundary line was surveyed, and mile points on the line from the Hudson River to the Delaware River were marked by sandstone monuments. The original 21st milestone has disappeared and has been replaced by a granite marker. This marker is extant but has been vandalized, and it is difficult to find.

Continue northward along the old mine road for another 925 feet until you reach a branch road which comes in from the right. Turn right and follow this side road to the east for a distance of approximately 375 feet to the mines.

The Snyder Mine is located about 120 feet to the north of the east-west woods road. It consists of a large open pit, now water-filled, about 100 feet in length. Numerous piles of rock ore are present along the west and south sides of this large open pit. An unusual feature is a platform or wall constructed of rock-ore which has been carefully stacked or laid-up along the western edge of the pit. There are several other test holes to the north and south of the main opening and several piles of ore.

The Snyder Mine was discovered by the Ogdens of Ringwood, who purchased the land in 1740 and noted the presence of iron deposits on the surface. By 1835, this mine had been worked to a length of about 100 feet and to a depth of twenty-five feet. The ore from this mine was sulphurous and produced iron of poor quality. This mine was abandoned some time well before 1889. The nearby road was a tram road which ran from the Peter's Mine in Ringwood.

The Hewitt Mine is located about fifty feet south of the woods road, opposite the Snyder Mine. This mine consists of a large open pit, also partially filled with water. It is 175 feet in length and about twenty-feet wide. There is one small rectangu-

> **The Hewitt Mine was opened before 1868 and consists of a large open pit, partially filled with water**

lar shaped exploratory hole located to the south of the main opening, and numerous ore piles are located nearby.

The Hewitt Mine is also located on land purchased by the Ogdens in 1740. This mine was opened before 1868 and was again worked in 1880. The ore vein ranged in thickness from six to twelve feet and was worked to a depth of twenty-five feet.

Hope and Peter's Mines

After visiting the Snyder and Hewitt Mines described above, return to the main mine road. Continue following the mine road in a northwesterly direction. Maintain a steady course on the mine road, which soon turns west and then begins to descend. Notice that the overhead power lines are off to the left of the road. The mine road then passes underneath the power lines. Here, the power line maintenance road comes in from the left and ends at the mine road. Continue straight ahead (west) on the mine road. In another 1,000 feet, you will pass under the power lines for a second time. In about 500 feet from the second power line crossing, you will come to a stream which crosses under the mine road through a culvert. Note the laid-up stone work on the side of the stream on your right and the corrugated metal pipe on your left. Just beyond this point, the mine road turns southwest and crosses back over the New York-New Jersey state line into Ringwood. Continue following the old mine road. Very soon it turns in a southerly direction and extends along the bottom of Hope Mountain, which lies to the right or west of the road. This road was once used extensively for carting ore from the Hope and Peter's Mines to the blast furnace at Ringwood.

The Hope Mine complex (figure 23) is situated along the eastern slope of Hope (formerly Wales) Mountain. As you proceed south along the mine road, the road emerges from the forest into a clear area. There are two wooden power line poles and a large metal power line pole to your left at the edge of the tree canopy. Directly opposite this point (which is about 750 feet beyond the stream culvert), on the right-hand side of the mine road, is a wide branch road that extends up the hillside. Follow this branch road uphill for 300 feet; note evidence of former mining activity on both sides. After 300 feet, turn right and walk about sixty feet to a chain-link fence which encloses the main shaft of the Hope Mine. Today, the Hope Mine complex consists of one large, deep water-filled pit on the side of the mountain and several shallow exploratory pits and trenches nearby. There are tailing piles or ore dumps along the steep mountainside as well. A trench, seventy-five feet long, ten feet wide and four feet deep, extends from the main mine road up the hillside just to the south of the branch road to the Hope Mine. Dry-laid stonework is visible along the length of this trench. This feature may be

Figure 24: Photograph of Peter's Mine, c. 1920s. Note small shaft in center which was dug in the 1760s by Peter Hasenclever's miners. (Courtesy of Louis P. West, Sr.)

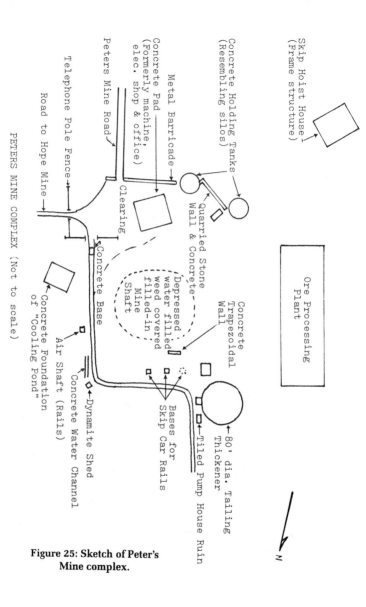

Figure 25: Sketch of Peter's Mine complex.

Skip Hoist House (Frame structure)

Concrete Holding Tanks (Resembling silos)

Metal Barricade

Concrete Pad (Formerly machine, elec. shop & office)

Peters Mine Road

Telephone Pole Fence

Road to Hope Mine

PETERS MINE COMPLEX (Not to scale)

Clearing

Quarried Stone Wall & Concrete

Concrete Base

Depressed water filled weed covered filled-in Mine Shaft

Concrete Trapezoidal Wall

Ore Processing Plant

Concrete Foundation of "Cooling Pond"

Air Shaft (Rails)

Concrete Water Channel

Dynamite Shed

Bases for Skip Car Rails

Tiled Pump House Ruin

80' dia. Tailing Thickener

N

the outer extent of a tunnel which, according to Edward Ringwood Hewitt, was driven into the hill to draw off the water from the nearby Hope Mine.

The main Hope Mine opening is presently fenced-in, and extreme caution must be exercised in approaching and viewing this mine. The mine is about 100 feet long and fifty feet deep, and is filled with water. It is an awesome and eerie cavern to behold and evokes images of the difficult and dangerous task of extracting hard rock ores from deep beneath the earth. During a recent visit to this mine, this author and a companion were startled by the sound of human groans coming from deep within the pit. Upon investigating these sounds, we saw what appeared to be a human head and hand alternately rising from and disappearing into the water at the bottom of the mine. This chilling experience convinced us that the ghost of a former miner still prowls the earth and shafts below our feet. Our associates saw nothing.

The old road at the base of Hope Mountain and the Hope Mine once contained narrow-gauge tracks on which mine cars operated. The tracks extended in a southerly direction, and the cars carried ore to the railroad line at Ringwood,

> **The Hope Mine is an awesome and eerie cavern evoking images of mining's difficulty**

near Margaret King Avenue. Although the tracks no longer exist, pieces of iron hardware, nails and steel cable, as well as ore, can be found within and along the road-bed.

The series of openings known as the Hope Mine was discovered and initially worked in 1767-1768. The ore was shipped to the Long Pond Ironworks where it was converted to a fine quality bar iron. However, the ore vein which had been opened and mined in five places was abandoned by the early 1780s. The mines were acquired by Martin Ryerson in 1807 and reopened shortly thereafter, but were shut down once again by 1836. One opening, referred to as the Oak Mine, was worked in 1845, but by 1867 all work at the Hope Mine had ceased.

From the Hope Mine openings, continue walking along the old tram road in a south-southwesterly direction for about one-half mile to the site of the Peter's Mine. The mine itself no longer exists, having been filled in, but the foundations and ruins of the Peter's Mine ore processing plant structures can still be seen and explored. These structures are decaying, crumbling and dangerous and should be viewed from a safe distance.

The Peter's Mine shaft, which once had seventeen work levels and extended underground some 3,000 feet, is now a debris-filled over-grown depression (figure 25). After passing through an opening in a log fence, turn right, recross the fence, and continue along an old road which leads through the remains of the Peter's Mine complex. On the right, you will observe the concrete foundation of the cooling pond. After about 200 feet, you will come to the remains of the emergency escape shaft for the mine. They are located about 50 feet to the right of the road, and are not visible from the road. The square concrete vertical shaft is now filled with water. It is covered with rails (and in part with chain-link fencing), and is partially surrounded by a broken-down fence. Return to the road and continue for another 200 feet. Here, to the right of the road, you will notice a small dynamite storage house (figure 27) measuring six and one-half by six and one-half feet in plan. This structure has wooden walls eight inches thick which are covered with sheet metal on the outside, and a hipped roof with an air vent. The dynamite storage house has two entrances, one on the north and one on the south, and two interior compart-ments with shelves.

At the northwestern end of the Peter's Mine complex, above the road, is a circular concrete tank-like structure eighty feet in diameter, which is identified on a 1943 map as a "tailing thickener." To the north of this structural feature is a concrete "lump ore bin" and piers of conveyor #7. To the

Figure 26: Photograph of Peter's Mine, Ringwood, New Jersey, c. early 1900s. (Terhune Collection; courtesy of North Jersey Highlands Historical Society.)

south of the tailing thickener is a small concrete overflow tank and a somewhat larger "hydro" tank with an adjacent grit bin. Along the hillside on the west are the ruins of the ore crushing plant. A large and imposing concrete skeleton — the remains of the ore concentrator plant — stands along the hillside west of the mine. Finally, at the southwestern side of the mine complex stands a wood-frame skip hoist house and the ruins of a skipway which once descended into the mine.

Two concrete storage tanks are also present in this area. All of these structures were built during World War II.

The Peter's Mine complex is strewn with structural debris. Much of the site is overgrown with trees, brush and poison ivy. Again, caution is the key word when hiking through this area.

Adjacent to the Peter's Mine complex are private homes which were once occupied by miners who worked at this and other nearby mines. The older miners' homes were modernized several years ago and no longer retain their historic appearance. Hikers should not trespass on private property and should respect the privacy of the area's residents.

The Peter's Mine was opened around 1740 and soon became the most productive of the Ringwood group of mines. It operated intermittently for over 200 years and has a fascinating history.

Prior to and during the Revolutionary War, the Peter's Mine supplied ore to the furnaces at Long Pond and Ringwood. However, by 1783 the mine was abandoned, and was not reopened until 1807, when the ironworks property was acquired by Martin Ryerson. By 1837, about 50,000 tons of ore had been removed from the mine. The mine was worked both as an open pit and by means of

**Figure 27:
Drawing of
dynamite storage
building,
Peter's Mine
complex, 1994.**

shafts extending from different levels.

In 1853, the Ringwood tract, including the mines and the Long Pond Ironworks, were purchased by Cooper & Hewitt, a managing company and agent for the Trenton Iron Company. Once again, the Peter's Mine was worked on and off during the Cooper & Hewitt period of ownership as economic needs dictated. By 1896, the Peter's Mine shaft extended to a depth of 800 feet. In 1900, nearly 19,000 tons of ore were removed from the mine, and on the ninth level a tunnel was dug to Hope Mountain extending the ore zone some 2,500 feet (figure 24). The mine was worked on and off until 1931, when all operations were closed down.

The Peter's Mine lay dormant and abandoned until 1942 when it was purchased by the United States Government. The Federal government proceeded to rehabilitate the Peter's Mine to make use of the ore during World War II. The old structures built in the mid-1800s were torn down, new ones were built, and the mine was dewatered, a task that required seven months to complete. In 1944, the government reported that there were seventeen levels in the mine and the shaft extended 2,400 feet to a depth of 1,800 feet below ground. The entrance to the

The Peter's Mine opened around 1740 and was the most productive of the Ringwood group

mine was widened and rebuilt with concrete. New structures and operations were added to the mine complex, including a new mill, a magnetic concentrating building, and an electric hoist. Nearly $4 million was spent on repairing the Ringwood Mines, but they operated only briefly during World War II.

In 1947, the government sold the mines to a new company known as Ringwood Mines, Inc., but in less than a year ownership reverted back to the government. Shortly thereafter, the mine was purchased by the Petroleum Export-Import Corporation of New York, but again the government took back ownership when this company's operations failed. In 1951, the mines were sold to a group known as Ringwood Iron Mines, Inc., for $1.5 million. This company planned to produce powdered and pelletized iron, but within three years they were out of business, and the property was again seized by the government in 1955. However, in 1956 the Borough of Ringwood foreclosed on the property for back taxes, put it up for sale and sold it back to the Federal government for nearly $1.7 million. Two years later, the government sold the property once again, this time to the Pittsburgh & Pacific Company.

The Pittsburgh & Pacific Company of Minnesota soon determined that it was uneconomical to reopen the mines. By 1961, all the machinery, iron rails, and other mining equipment was put up for sale.

In 1964, the J.I. Kislak Realty Company, representing the Ringwood Realty Company, purchased the property from Pittsburgh & Pacific. The Ringwood Realty Company proposed to seal the mine entrances and build a $50 million self-contained community, but this project was never developed. Instead, the Ringwood Realty Company proceeded to fill the mines with waste from the Ford Motor Company Assembly Plant in Mahwah, New Jersey. In the early 1970s, the Ringwood Realty Company donated much of the mine area land to the Borough of Ringwood.

Today, nearly all traces of the mine shaft are gone. As you stand on the road and look around, the only visible

By 1961, the machinery, iron rails, and other mining equipment were put up for sale

remnants of the mine are the skeletal ruins of the structures built by the government in the 1940s.

Before returning to Ringwood Manor, the historical hiker should contemplate the magnitude of the mines in the Ringwood area. In addition to the Hope and Peter's Mines, numerous other mine openings existed in the area, together with workers' houses and other structures. One of the oldest and, perhaps, most important of the Ringwood group of mines was the Cannon Mine. This mine was located about one mile south of the Peter's Mine. It was worked intermittently from 1763 to 1931. The Cannon Mine consisted of four veins of ore which were worked along four levels, reaching a total vertical depth of about 500 feet. On the surface, the mine was a large open pit that extended to a depth of 200 feet. A hoisting tower stood nearby. Today, little can be seen of the Cannon Mine. The open pit has been filled in and is now a weed-filled depression. The hoist is gone, but piles of ore are present. Its name survives as a street sign, "Cannon Mine Road."

To continue your iron mine trails journey, return to the modern paved road, known as Peter's Mine Road, and walk south along the road. To your right, along the hillside, are many of the former miners' homes. Although these homes have been recently modernized and other physical improvements have been made, the Ringwood Mines area still presents a view of mining life in the Ramapos.

After about 1,400 feet, you will reach an intersection with Cable House Road, with the Borough of Ringwood recycling area on your right. Continue south on Peter's

---

Today, nearly all traces of the Peter's mine shaft are gone

Mine Road, passing several driveways to the right, until you reach a second paved road which comes in from the right. (This intersection is approximately 1,200 feet south of the junction with Cable House Road). About 280 feet south of this second junction, you will come to the unmarked AT&T underground cable crossing. This right-of-way is clear and open at all times. Turn left and follow the AT&T right-of-way uphill to the east. At the top of the hill, you will encounter the clearly marked Blue Trail. Turn right and follow this hiking trail in a southerly direction. After proceeding south along the Blue Trail for about 0.4 mile, the observant hiker will notice the remains of a wrought iron twisted-strand cable within the trail. This one-and-one-quarter-inch diameter cable extends for about 120 feet along the trail.

In 1858, Peter Cooper of the Trenton Iron Company attempted to construct a gravity conveyor system to transport iron ore in buckets from the Ringwood Mines to Boardville, a distance of three miles. The system consisted of a continuous iron cable which passed around a large drum at each end with the cable supported above ground by means of poles located sixty feet apart. Buckets, each containing 160 pounds of ore, suspended off the ground would carry the ore downgrade to the forge site. However, there is no evidence to indicate that this system was ever put into successful operation. The length of wrought iron cable found along the Blue Trail may be a remnant of Peter Cooper's gravity conveyor system of 1858. Alternatively, the cable may be from other mining operations and simply discarded here.

By 1880, a tram road was in operation carrying ore from the mines to a railroad junction at Ringwood. Ore-filled cars traveled by gravity along narrow-gauge tracks to the rail head. The cars were guided and braked by young boys who often enjoyed a wild downhill ride. A "dinky" steam engine pushed the filled ore cars to the top of the hill and later pulled the empty cars back to the mine (figure 21). The Blue Trail now utilizes part of the old tram road.

Continue along the Blue Trail, which now curves to the right. In another 0.4 mile, you will come to a junction. Bear left, and continue along an old estate road, now marked with both blue and intermittent red blazes. You will pass a pond and an old cemetery on the right. After the road curves to the right, you will reach a junction where the Blue Trail turns left. You should recognize this spot from the beginning of the hike. Continue straight ahead on the road, passing the manor house to the right, and you will soon see the parking area ahead.

Roomy Mine

*T*his mine (figure 28), formerly known as the Laurel or Red Mine, is situated about half a mile south of Snake Den Road in the Borough of Ringwood, New Jersey. To reach the Roomy Mine, take West Brook Road to Snake Den Road. Proceed to the end of the road, and park in the large parking area of the Weis Ecology Center on the right side. Walk back along the road for 150 feet and turn right, following the red blazes of the Wyanokie Circular Trail and the yellow blazes of the Mine Trail. After 0.2 mile, when the yellow blazes turn off to the

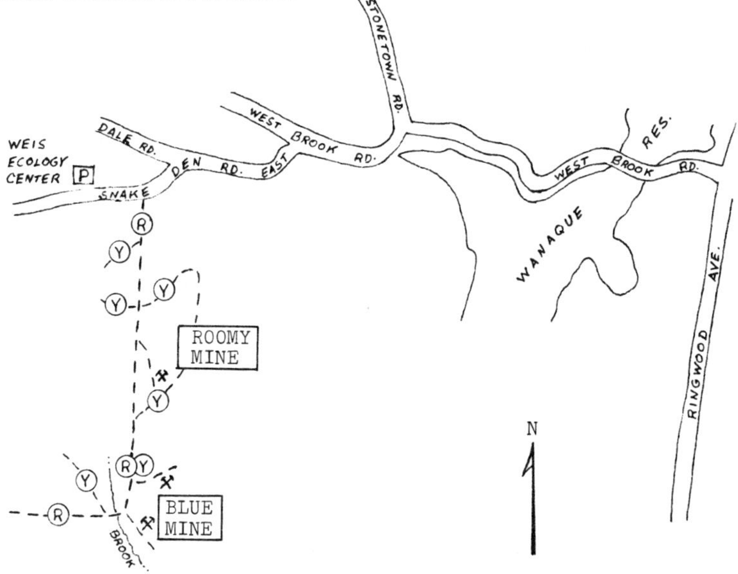

Figure 28: Map showing locations of Roomy and Blue Mines.

Key:
⚒ - Mine/Test
Ⓡ - Red Trail
Ⓨ - Yellow Trail
P - Parking

right, continue straight ahead, following the red blazes. The yellow trail will cross the red trail in another 600 feet; again, continue straight ahead on the red trail. About 400 feet beyond this point, you will notice an unmarked trail going off to the left. This is an old, narrow mine road which was used to transport iron ore from the Roomy Mine. Turn left and follow this road for about 600 feet to the mine. A large tailings dump is present directly in front of the entrance.

The Roomy Mine can be entered. A large interior chamber is accessible and from this chamber a low, horizontal adit and shaft can be followed for about 100 feet into the hillside. A hard hat is recommended, as rock can fall from the roof. A flashlight is absolutely necessary for exploring the adit and horizontal shaft. Extreme caution should be used at all times of the year — ice, mud, and water can be present. Climbing from the interior chamber to the top of the opening on the hillside is ill-advised as this can loosen rock and cause further collapse of the mine.

For a good view of an upper opening to the mine, climb up the yellow Mine Trail, which joins the mine road just beyond the mine entrance. A further climb to the top of the hill on the yellow trail will reward the

---

The Roomy Mine is an excellent mine to visit early in your explorations of old mine trails

---

hiker with a beautiful view of the surrounding hills. There are also several mine pits and ore piles along this section of the yellow trail, and on the hilltop above the Roomy Mine.

The Roomy Mine is an excellent mine to visit early in your explorations of old mine trails. It is an easy hike from the parking lot of the Weis Ecology Center on Snake Den Road to this mine. The mine itself is both spectacular and informative. As you climb the narrow road to the mine, consider how it might have been used to remove ore. Was it wider? Were mules used rather than wagons? Observe the staging area in front of the mine entrance. Tailings have been used to provide a large, level area for mining equipment and loading ore to haul away.

Stand before the mine entrance and note how the entrance, twenty-five feet long and about five feet wide, has been cut into the hillside. Find the drill holes and drill marks. At the mine face, you will see two sizeable holes. The upper one, which looks into the large chamber and vertical shaft, is not easily accessible. This hole was opened from both the inside and the outside of the mine. This is *not* the way into the mine. Instead, to your left you will see a lower opening, now rock filled and about two and a half feet high and five feet wide. Crawl through this opening.

You will find yourself in a large chamber twenty-five feet square, open to the sky through an angled shaft some fifty feet long. The first opening, which you observed from the entrance, is apparent on a ledge halfway up the shaft. This may have been an earlier level for the removal

of rock and ore. Numerous drill marks appear on the walls of the shaft and chamber. They are all about fifteen to seventeen inches long and about one and one-fourth inches in diameter. Standing at the bottom of the shaft, you can see in these drill marks the pattern in which this shaft was dug from the top. Metal drills were hammered into the bedrock. The holes were drilled four to six feet apart. Packed with black powder, they were detonated, and large chunks of rock were loosened and

---

You will find yourself in a large chamber twenty-five feet square and open to the sky

---

carted away. Possibly, this shaft held a good vein of ore, now removed.

You will have noticed a second feature leading away from this chamber. Directly opposite the hole you crawled in through is the rectangular opening of the adit. Some rock rubble is strewn at the entrance, but the adit is five and a half feet high and six feet wide.

Watch your head, use your hardhat and flashlight, and follow this tunnel. You will notice a temperature change: it is constantly about fifty two degrees in here — warm on a cold day and cool on a hot one. Examine the wall and roof surfaces for drill marks and other signs of how the adit and the second chamber were carved out. Consider the human labor spent in burrowing deep into the rock. Consider a long, hard day's work down in the mine, with the ringing of hammer on drill, the noise and rock flying in explosion, the hard labor of mucking out the shattered rock. Deep within the hillside, you are standing in hand-made, man-made space.

Opened shortly after 1840, the Roomy Mine was worked until about 1857. It lay dormant for over thirty years and was then re-explored about 1890. The ore was compact, and free from rock. The ore vein measured about four feet thick and dipped sharply to the southeast. The Roomy Mine is named after Benjamin Roome, a local 19th century land surveyor.

Blue Mine

Visit the Blue Mine (figure 28) on the same hike as the Roomy Mine for a contrasting view of mining in this area. There are two principal mine openings which can be examined. To reach the Blue Mine from the Roomy Mine, proceed south on the yellow-blazed Mine Trail, which follows the route of the old road to the mine. In about 650 feet, the yellow trail joins the red-blazed Wyanokie Circular Trail. Turn left and follow the joint red-and-yellow trail south for about 0.2 mile. At this point, you will notice an unmarked but well-worn trail going off to the left. Follow this trail, which has rectangular sheet-metal strips nailed to trees at intervals along its route, for about 800 feet, at which point you will encounter a large pile of mine rock adjacent to the trail. Scramble up this ore pile to a flat, work-staging area of a large mine trench nearby. This trench is fifty feet long, twenty-five feet wide and fifteen feet deep, and is filled with water. After viewing this mine opening, retrace your steps to the joint red-and-yellow trail. Continue south on the red-and-yellow trail to a wooden footbridge which crosses Blue Mine Brook. Do not cross the bridge; instead, continue straight ahead for 100 feet, and you will see the Blue Mine on the left.

The Blue Mine — which is also known as the London, Iron Hill or Whynockie Mine — undoubtedly received its common name from the varying dark blue color of its ore. This ore deposit was first discovered and opened by Peter Hasenclever around 1765. Hasenclever was the ironmaster of the American or London Company, which operated blast furnaces and forges at Ringwood, Long Pond, and Charlotteburg in New Jersey. Thus, it was first known as the London Mine.

During the early 19th century, the mine was worked by Peter M. Ryerson and the ore was shipped to the Freedom Furnace in Midvale, New Jersey. The furnace, also known as Ryerson's or Whynockie Furnace, went "out of blast"

or shut down in 1855.

In 1868, the Blue Mine was examined by the New Jersey Geological Survey, which reported that it had been worked for a distance of 150 feet. The ore vein was nine to ten feet thick, its dip was perpendicular and it pitched fifty-eight degrees to the northeast. Later, the mine extended 500 feet in length and the ore body was sixteen feet wide. The ore was

---

The Blue Mine received its name from the dark blue color of its ore

---

described as hard, compact, and containing hornblende, mica and rock. The ore also contained a considerable amount of sulphur, which was an undesirable ingredient that caused iron to become brittle when it was heated and worked.

The Blue Mine was reopened in 1871, worked for two years and closed. It was reopened again in 1886 by the Whynockie Iron Company, but was operated for only a short period of time. In 1890 it was again reopened,

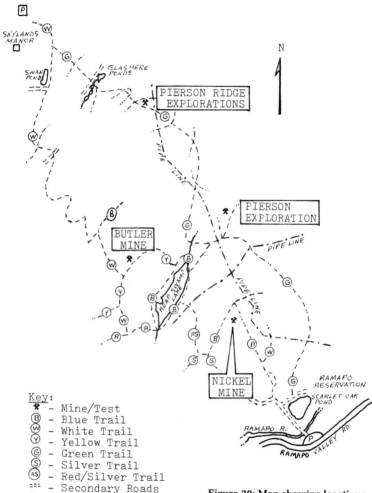

Key:
✱ - Mine/Test
Ⓑ - Blue Trail
Ⓦ - White Trail
Ⓨ - Yellow Trail
Ⓖ - Green Trail
Ⓢ - Silver Trail
⒭Ⓢ - Red/Silver Trail
≡≡≡ - Secondary Roads
P - Parking

Figure 29: Map showing locations
of Butler and Nickel Mines,
Pierson Exploration
and Pierson Ridge Explorations.

and a gang of twenty miners raised over 8,000 tons of ore from the shaft. The Midvale Mining Company operated three boilers and two hoisting and pumping engines at the site. This company also built two ore roasters near the mine to heat the ore to drive off the sulphur. Further processing included the removal of waste rock, after which the ore contained fifty-four percent iron. However, once again the mine was shut down. Finally, it was reopened in 1905 and dewatered, but no ore was taken out.

Today, the Blue Mine is filled with water. Since the ore body was nearly perpendicular, the mine shaft would constantly fill up with water, which had to be pumped out each time it was reopened. During its early period of operation, a waterwheel was used to provide power to operate the pumps used to dewater the mine. Water power may also have been used to operate the mine hoist. A large concrete pad is located immediately in front of the mine and at one time functioned as a base for equipment, possibly the steam-operated hoisting or pumping engines. The remains of stone foundations are present nearby, and large piles of mine tailings are located on the hillside and hilltop surrounding the mine.

The remains of an earthen dam and a banked stone foundation are located on Blue Mine Brook to the northwest of the mine. To find these features, hike upstream from the wooden footbridge along the easterly side of the brook. After traveling about 150 feet, you will see the banked structure, a well-preserved ruin of a powder magazine, on your right. Continue hiking upstream for another 200 feet and you will encounter the remains of the dam on both sides of the brook.

Butler Mine

The Butler Mine (figure 29) is located on a high ridge just west of Bear Swamp Lake in the Township of Mahwah, Bergen County, New Jersey. The mine is situated along the yellow-blazed Hoeferlin Trail, just north of its intersection with the Crossover Trail. To reach the Butler Mine, park in

Lot A at the Skylands Manor section of Ringwood State Park and proceed south on the white-blazed Crossover Trail. Climb steadily uphill on this scenic trail, passing Swan Pond and Gatum Pond, and soon reaching the southern end of the Pierson Ridge. Continue along the white trail in a southeast direction to its junction with the yellow-blazed Hoeferlin Trail. Turn left (north) on the yellow trail, and proceed for about 500 feet to the mine site, which is on the left (west) side of the trail.

The Butler Mine was worked prior to 1868 and was the scene of extensive exploration work. The excavation of pits and trenches uncovered a vein of good quality ore 120 feet long and five to eleven feet in width. On lower ground fifty feet southwest of this opening is a second cut fourteen feet wide and dug to a depth of seven feet, which revealed ore, much of which was pure. Seventy feet to the southwest is a third cut or trench which had an ore vein eleven feet thick. Most of the exploratory work was done in 1873-1874 and 1879, during which fifty

tons of ore were removed from the site by R.F. Galloway of Suffern, New York. The Butler Mine was re-opened in 1880 and worked for only a month, during which it produced 280 tons of iron ore. The mine has been abandoned since then.

Pierson Exploration

A small mine exploration hole is located just west of a woods road, formerly the route of the yellow-blazed Hoeferlin Trail, a short distance to the northeast of Bear Swamp Lake in the Township of Mahwah, Bergen County, New Jersey (figure 29). The mine is situated within the Ramapo Valley County Reservation, originally the southeast corner of property belonging to the Ramapo Land Company.

To reach the Pierson Exploration, park at the entrance to the Ramapo Valley County Reservation on Route 202, and proceed west on the main park road, the Silver Trail. Follow the Silver Trail as it passes to the left of Scarlet Oak Pond and then bears left and begins to ascend. After about a mile and half, where the Silver Trail makes a sharp left turn, continue straight ahead on the Red-Silver Trail. Follow the Red-Silver Trail until it ends at the blue-blazed Shore Trail, along the shore of Bear Swamp Lake, then turn right onto the Shore Trail. You will note that the Shore Trail follows a wide dirt road. In

---

The "mud spoon" was used to remove bits of rock from drill holes before blasting

---

another quarter of a mile, the road bears right, away from the lake shore, while the trail goes ahead on a footpath. At this point, leave the trail and continue along the road. Soon the green-blazed Halifax Trail joins from the left. About 750 feet beyond this point, you will reach a gas pipeline. Here the wide dirt road bends to the right. Continue straight ahead for another 100 feet, following the green markers, and you will come to a triple junction. The main woods road curves to the left, while the green trail goes straight

ahead on another woods road. Between the green trail and the main woods road, a third road goes off to the north. The beginning of this road is marked by a blacked-out triple blaze on a tree. This road, which was the former route of the Hoeferlin Trail, is the one you should take. As you proceed north on this road, you may notice some faded yellow blazes. Continue for about 1,100 feet along the road, and you will see the mine opening on the hillside to the left (west) of the road, about 50 feet from the road.

This mine hole measures eighteen feet in length by twelve feet in width and is about three feet

Figure 30: Drawing of brass mud spoon found at Pierson Exploration.

deep. There is a quantity of quarried stone blocks and fragments on the south side of the pit, and several one-and-one-half-inch diameter drill holes are present in the west wall of the hole, as well as on several stone blocks. No iron ore was extracted from this opening. The Pierson Exploration dates back to before 1862, since it is shown on an 1862 map of the Pierson Estate.

During a 1988 archaeological survey, a brass wire "mud spoon" — two feet long and one-eighth of an inch in diameter — was found in the Pierson Exploration pit (figure 30). One end of the wire is flattened, presenting a spatula-like termination. This tool was used to remove bits of rock from the drill holes as they were being cut in preparation for blasting.

For an alternate return route to the parking area, you can turn left (east) on the green-blazed Halifax Trail and follow it back to its end at Scarlet Oak Pond. A right turn on the dirt road which runs along the pond will take you back to the Silver Trail, and a left turn on that trail will bring you to the parking area where you started the hike.

Nickel Mine

This mine (figure 29) is located on Monroe Ridge in the Ramapo Valley County Reservation, in the Township of Mahwah, Bergen County, New Jersey. The mine lies between Green Mountain Valley (a.k.a. Havemeyer Hollow) on the north and MacMillan Reservoir, just west of the Ridge Trail. The mine is situated on a flat terrace just below and west of the brow of Monroe Ridge. There is a moderate rise to the north of the mine, a steep rise to the east, and a sharp drop to the west.

To reach the Nickel Mine, take the Silver Trail west from the parking area of the Ramapo Valley County Reservation on Route 202. This trail — a wide dirt road — passes to the left of Scarlet Oak Pond, then curves left and begins to climb. After approximately three-fourths of a mile, the blue-blazed Ridge Trail goes off to the right. Turn right and continue along the Ridge Trail as it switchbacks up the steep hillside, following an old road to the top of Monroe

Ridge. Just before reaching the top, a side trail to the left leads to a beautiful lookout, from which New York City can be seen. About 600 feet beyond the lookout side trail, continue on the Ridge Trail as it bears left, leaving the road. As the trail reaches the ridgetop, you will note a stone fence or wall to the right or east of the trail. The Ridge Trail continues in a northwest direction, close to the western brow of the hill, with some slight descents and ascents. After about half a mile along the ridgetop, the Ridge Trail joins an old road which comes in from the right. At this junction, turn off the trail and proceed 250 degrees west-southwest downhill for about 275 feet to the mine.

Two pits are present at this mine, and there is a trace of a road or trail to the south of them. One pit is a circular vertical hole, about fifteen feet in diameter, now filled with water and surrounded by large piles of tailings. A shallow ditch extends westerly from the northwest side of the pit. There is a second oval-shaped pit forty feet to the west. This pit is about ten feet long and six feet deep, and is also filled with water. Quarried rock is evident throughout the area, and a few drill holes, one and one-quarter inches in diameter, are visible.

Tradition associates the Nickel Mine with the Hopkins and Dickinson

---

A side trail leads to a lookout from which New York City can be seen

---

Manufacturing Company, which was located nearby along the Ramapo River. Hopkins and Dickinson operated at Darlington from 1872 to 1881. During this period, this company undertook a search for nickel-bearing rock in the mountains to the west of their operations. Ore was found on Monroe Ridge, where some drilling and digging was done, but no mining was carried out. The Hopkins and Dickinson Manufacturing Company produced bronze fittings, locks, and iron castings for residential, commercial, and public buildings.

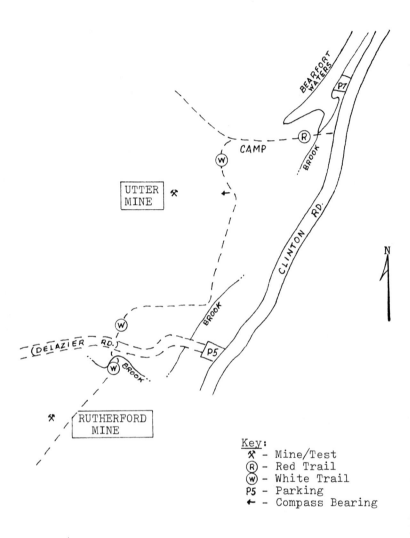

Figure 31: Map showing locations of Rutherford and Utter Mines.

Pierson Ridge Explorations

Three exploratory pits are located on the south side of an old woods road on Pierson Ridge in Ringwood State Park, just across the Bergen County border in the Township of Mahwah, New Jersey. These mine pits lie twenty feet south of the road and 140 feet west of the Tennessee Gas transmission pipeline (figure 29).

To reach these explorations, park in Lot A at the Skylands Manor section of Ringwood State Park and proceed east and then south on the white-blazed Crossover Trail. In about a third of a mile, turn left on the green-blazed Halifax Trail, which switchbacks up Mount Defiance on an old carriage road. At the top, it crosses the red-blazed Ringwood-Ramapo Trail and then descends to a wide woods road at Glasmere Ponds. After crossing between the ponds on the road, follow the green trail as it bears left, leaving the road, and begins to ascend Pierson Ridge.

Further up, the trail crosses the road twice in a short distance, cutting across a switchback on the road. At the third road crossing, turn left onto the road, and continue for 300 feet to the mine openings, which are on the right (south) side of the road.

The three pits are circular exploration holes. The largest pit, which is nearest the road, measures twenty-three feet in diameter and is twelve feet deep. The other two pits — located south of the largest pit — are fifteen feet in diameter and are about five feet deep. Rock tailings are present in the immediate vicinity of each hole. It is not known when these explorations were dug or by whom.

Rutherford Mine

The Rutherford Mine (figure 31) consists of three deep shafts, two open trenches and several exploratory pits located along the northwesterly side of an old woods road which extends southerly from Delazier Road in West Milford

Township, New Jersey. Delazier Road begins at Clinton Road and connects with the road to the Rutherford Mine, running through Pequannock Watershed property and private land. (On the 1991 edition of Trail Conference Map #21, Delazier Road is shown as an unnamed woods road which runs west from parking area P5 on Clinton Road.) A hiking permit is required and

---

__The Rutherford Mine has deep water-filled shafts surrounded by large tailing piles__

---

can be obtained from the Newark Watershed Conservation and Development Corporation office on Echo Lake Road in West Milford.

To reach the mine, park at site P5 on Clinton Road, proceed west on Delazier Road, then turn left (south) on the first woods road you encounter. The first shaft can be found about one mile in from Clinton Road.

The mine shafts are deep, filled with water and surrounded by large piles of tailings. The remains of several structures, dry-laid stone foundations, are located nearby. The hiker must exercise extreme caution in approaching and observing these shafts. Barbed wire which once fenced off these pits is now a hazard which could trip the incautious observer. The shafts, trenches, pits and foundations are northeast of the old Standard Oil pipeline. This pipeline was constructed in 1881 and carried oil from Olean, New York, to Bayonne, New Jersey. It originally followed the New York, Susquehanna and Western Railroad through northern New Jersey. However, in 1916 a bypass was built to avoid the reservoirs in the Newark Watershed. The pipeline was abandoned in 1927. The route of the old pipeline, which can be easily seen, crosses the mountain ridges between Cherry Ridge and Cedar Pond.

The Rutherford Mine was first opened during the second quarter of the 19th century. The mine supplied ore to the Clinton Furnace, located nearby, which was in operation intermittently from 1826 to 1837. A great deal of exploratory work for ore deposits took place in the area. In 1888, a shaft was sunk on the Rutherford property to a depth of 100 feet, but it failed to discover a sizeable body of ore. About 1890, ore was mined for the Franklin Furnace in Franklin, New Jersey. However, mining operations ceased because of the high cost of transportation to that furnace.

Utter Mine

*T*he Utter Mine Lot (figure 31) extends along the crest of a hill which is located to the west of Clinton Road and south of Old Coal Road in West Milford Township, Passaic County, New Jersey. The mine openings are within the Pequannock Watershed, and a permit is required to hike on watershed property. Hiking permits can be obtained from the Newark Watershed Conservation and Development Corporation (NWCDC) office which is located on Echo Lake Road in West Milford, New Jersey.

The Utter Mine is named for the family of that name which owned land in this area. The 1861 Map of the County of Passaic, New Jersey, shows the location of several dwellings, identified as belonging to several Utter family members, along Clinton Road in the area between the Old Coal Road on the north and Stephens Road on the south. Later historic maps identify this general area as the hamlet of Uttertown.

The Utter Mine openings are located along a densely wooded hilltop in what was at one time open farm fields or pasture. A hike to find this site is challenging, as there is no direct trail to the mine. However, the adventurous hiker will be rewarded by the experience of seeing and *feeling* the extant remains of hardscrabble farming in the Highlands, as well as the mine openings themselves.

A hikers' parking area — designated as P7 — is located on the west side of Clinton Road near the lake or pond called Bearfort Waters. Park there and walk south along the west side of Clinton Road a short distance to Old Coal Road (now a red-blazed trail). Turn right and head west along the road, passing through a camp area. Just beyond the camp buildings you will reach a fork in the road. Take the road to the left which extends along the base of a hill on your right. (The right fork is the Old Coal Road which continues uphill; do *not* take this route.) Proceed southwesterly along the road, crossing a small brook and the route of an abandoned gas pipeline. As you proceed south along the trail, scan the

---

A hike to the Utter Mine is challenging, as there is no direct trail going to the site

---

hillside to your right (west) and look for a vertical cliff face.

You will notice a small flat area directly in front of the cliff, and a side trail which makes a short loop up to and over this plateau and back down to the main trail. At this point, take a due west compass bearing and head through the woods, around the cliff and up the hillside to the Utter Mine Lot. Note the presence of stone walls or fences extending along the

hillside. At the top of the hill, there are ten stone piles or heaps. These are the result of land clearing activities when this area was being used as pasture for the grazing of animals.

There are three mine openings, all exploratory pits, located along the top of the hill. The first is a rectangular opening which is located just west of the stone piles and below the brow of the hill. This mine pit measures twenty-six feet in length, sixteen feet in width, and eight feet in depth. Small backfill piles are present around the opening.

A second mine pit is located about 300 feet north of the one just described. This exploratory pit is circular, measuring twenty-four feet in diameter and ten feet in depth. Some mine tailings are present adjacent to this pit, and traces of a stone foundation are present about eighty feet north of the pit. This foundation wall consists of two courses of stone ten feet long, but the width of the structure is undetermined. Although the nature of this ruin is unknown, its size and location suggest that it was a small structure associated with the Utter Mine openings.

A third mine pit is located about 300 feet north of the circular pit. This opening is also a rectangular exploratory mine pit which measures twenty-six feet in length, sixteen feet in width, and six feet in depth. Mine tailings are present on the north and south sides of this opening.

The three exploratory pits of the Utter Mine were opened in the late 19th century by prospectors associated with Thomas A. Edison. A map of the Utter Mine Magnetic Belt in the State Geologist's Report of 1910 shows their prospecting efforts in this area. In 1888, Edison began construction of an iron ore separating and concentrating works in Ogdensburg, New Jersey. He sent out teams of prospectors-surveyors throughout New Jersey and New York to seek high-quality magnetite ore for his new enterprise. The ore in the Utter Mine, however, proved to be of poor quality, and the mine was not worked commercially.

Green Mine

The Green Mine (figure 32) is located along the east side of Wawayanda Road in Wawayanda State Park, about half a mile south of the New York-New Jersey state line. To reach this site, use the main park entrance off Warwick Turnpike, and leave your car in the visitor's parking area adjacent to the park office. Proceed north on the blue-blazed Hoeferlin Trail for 0.2 mile, then turn left on the white-blazed Appalachian Trail and follow it for 0.3 mile to Wawayanda Road, which is an unpaved park road. Turn right, leaving the blazed trail, and continue in a northerly direction along Wawayanda Road until you come to a road on your left, known as the Crossover Road. The Green Mine openings are situated just southeast of this intersection, on the east side of Wawayanda Road.

The site consists of a rectangular open shaft, ten feet by five feet and about fifty feet deep, and two former shafts that have been filled in by the park authorities. Exploratory pits are also

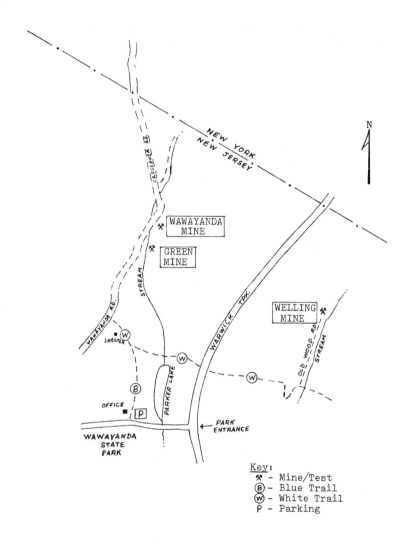

Figure 32: Map showing locations of Green, Wawayanda and Welling Mines.

present in the vicinity, along with several mine dumps or tailing piles and a stone base, probably the remains of an equipment platform, with brick fragments and coal. The foundation of a former mule barn is located southwest of the junction of the Crossover Road and Wawayanda Road, west of the Green Mine complex. This structure was a two-story bank barn, and the dry-laid stone foundation measures forty feet in length by twenty-five feet in width.

The Green Mine was opened by 1853 and consisted of three openings, with ore bodies measuring one foot, two feet, and four feet wide, respectively. The mine supplied ore to the Wawayanda Furnace, located nearby, which produced pig iron (cast iron) from 1846 to 1867. By 1868, several additional mine holes were opened to the southwest of the original three. The mine was not worked between 1868 and 1879. The Green Mine and the nearby Wawayanda Furnace were purchased by the Thomas Iron Company in 1869. The mine was reopened in 1880, operated for a short time,

shut down and reopened again in 1887, and then finally abandoned in 1888.

Wawayanda Mine

The Wawayanda Mine (figure 32) is located about 500 feet northeast of the Green Mine in Wawayanda State Park. The remains of this mine complex are extensive and include a partially filled shaft with cross-log cribbing, an open trench, exploratory pits, and tailing piles. The site also contains the remains of a semi-subterranean structure that may have functioned as a storage cellar for blasting powder. Other structural remains are present in the area, including stone retaining walls, derrick platforms and a banked barn foundation. Unfortunately, this site has been disturbed to a large extent by soil mining activities, attempts to fill the mine holes and recent 20th century trash dumping.

The Wawayanda Mine first opened in 1776, and its ore was shipped to forges in Warwick, New York. It was reopened in 1854 and consisted of five deposits of ore. One of these deposits had an ore vein that was two to eight feet wide, with a tunnel entrance, and was worked to a depth of sixty feet. A second ore body, two to twelve feet wide, was excavated fifty feet on each side of a tunnel, which itself was fifty feet below the surface. A third deposit was worked for about 105 feet along its strike and an adjoining branch for 100 feet.

In 1867, the mine property was purchased by the Thomas Iron Company, but apparently all mining activity had ceased and the openings had been abandoned. The mine was reopened and worked again between 1873 and 1877. It closed in 1877, but was reopened and worked from 1880 to 1881, shipping 4,700 tons of ore. In 1887, 1890 and 1891, it was operated once again, with about 450 tons of ore being shipped from the mine.

Warren D. Lewis, who was superintendent of Wawayanda State Park in the late 1960s and early 1970s, related a story told to him by old-timers who lived in the area all their lives that several men and mules were buried in this mine by a cave-in.

Welling Mine

The Welling Mine (figure 32) is located approximately one-half mile east of Warwick Turnpike in Vernon Township, New Jersey. The site can be reached by means of the Appalachian Trail heading east from the Warwick Turnpike. The Appalachian Trail goes through the woods and down a steep slope, at the bottom of which it crosses a stream. Near this point, an old woods road runs in a northerly direction. Turn left here and follow this road north for about 1,500 feet to the mine area. This road section was formerly part of the Appalachian Trail.

Four vertical shafts are visible along the road. Log cribbing is extant and clearly visible within two of these mine shafts. Shallow exploratory pits, as well as tailing piles, are also present in the area. To the west of these openings, and on top of the hill or ridge, were several other shafts, but these have been bulldozed and filled in.

The Welling Mine, also known as Ten Eyck's Exploration, was opened in 1855 at five locations along an ore deposit. The ore in these mine openings was lean, but some of it was sent to the Wawayanda Furnace. Additional exploratory openings were made between 1873 and 1876, and again in 1879. In 1879, 400 tons of ore were mined but reportedly never shipped. Despite a large investment of time, money and effort, the Welling Mine was not profitable.

Cole Farm Mine

*T*he Cole Farm Mine (figure 33) is located in the Borough of Kinnelon near its boundary with Montville Township in Morris County, New Jersey. The site is easily accessible to hikers by way of the new Pyramid Mountain Natural Historical Area Park.

To reach this mine, take Morris County Route 511 (Boonton Avenue) to the parking area at the Visitor's Center, opposite the Mars Industrial Park. The Visitor's Center is located about 0.8 mile north of Taylortown Road and a little over three miles north of Boonton. From the parking area, follow the access trail to the blue-blazed Mennen Trail, and continue west on the blue trail to its junction with the white-blazed Kinnelon-Boonton Trail. Bear left and follow the white trail north, passing the ruins of an abandoned farmstead. Continue along this trail, which parallels an old stone wall, until you reach Bear Rock. This huge glacially-deposited boulder, once the habitation site of prehistoric Indians, is situated on the Kinnelon-Montville border. A land survey mark is carved into the top surface of the rock.

To find the Cole Farm Mine, strike a compass bearing due west from Bear Rock. The route to the mine site is not a marked trail and will require you to cross a small stream and go around some steep, nearly vertical rock ledges, always maintaining a westerly course from Bear Rock. The route is uphill, with the mine situated on a small plateau on the easterly side of Stony Brook

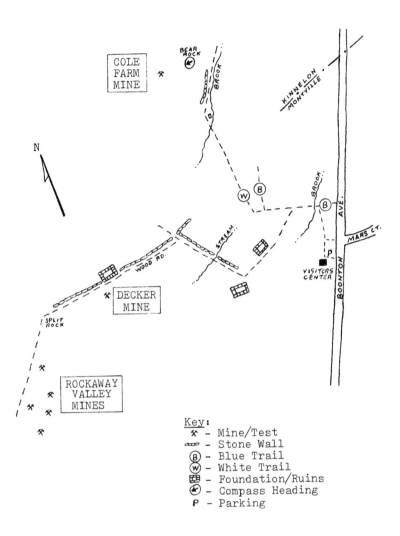

Figure 33: Map showing locations of Cole Farm, Decker and Rockaway Valley Mines.

Mountain, about 1,000 feet from Bear Rock.

The mine is a keyhole-shaped exploratory trench that is forty feet long, fifteen feet wide and five feet deep. The open trench is filled with leaves. A pile of mine tailings lies adjacent to the easterly and downslope side of the trench. The bedrock outcrop in the vicinity of the mine has a distinct black coloration, and it is undoubtedly this feature that lured iron ore prospectors to this area.

The 1910 geological survey of iron mines in New Jersey describes the site as an "exploration" that was opened in 1874. The iron deposit was found to be lean, that is, of low quality, and no further work was conducted at the site.

Decker Mine

*T*he Decker Mine (figure 33) is located about one mile southwest of the Cole Farm Exploration on the eastern slope of Stony Brook Mountain in Montville Township, New Jersey. It is situated on private property, so permis-

sion should be obtained from the landowner before beginning the hike.

The route to the Decker Mine begins on Morris County Route 511 (Boonton Avenue) at the Pyramid Mountain Visitor's Center.

The Decker Mine was opened in 1872 and consists of a 26-foot-long trench

---

From the parking area, follow the access trail to the blue-blazed Mennen Trail, and cross the stream which flows southerly from the Taylortown Reservoir. A short distance past the stream, an old woods road joins the blue trail on the left, while the blue trail continues uphill to the right. At this junction, turn left and follow the unmarked woods road in a southwest-erly direction. This road takes you past the stone foundation of a large barn on the right and leads to the site of a farmhouse. At this point, the road turns north-westerly and parallels a stone wall. Continue along the road, crossing a stream.

You will reach a large stone wall which joins the road at a right angle from the left and continues on the opposite side of the road. Turn sharply left here, and follow the road uphill, until you see the foundation of a structure on the right. The Decker Mine is opposite this ruin on the south side of the old road.

The house site at the Decker Mine is located on the north side of the road, immediately adjacent to a dry-laid stone retaining

---

The Rockaway Valley Mines are a complex of shafts, trenches, large open pits and work staging areas

---

wall. The foundation of the dwelling is thirty feet long and sixteen feet wide, with its long axis oriented north-south. The structure is divided into two sections, with a deep cellar hole and stair entry way on the north and a shallow crawl space on the south. There is a flat terrace adjoining the south-east side of the foundation that measures thirty-two feet

by twenty-six feet, with brick fragments on the surface. The remains of an earth-banked storage building or stone chamber are located twenty-two feet to the west of the house on a hillside. The interior of this dry-laid stone chamber measures fourteen feet by seven feet, and the intact stonework is three feet high.

The Decker Mine is located twenty-six feet south of the old road. It consists of an open trench twenty-six feet long, fourteen feet wide and four feet deep. Forty-three feet south of the trench there is a shallow explor-atory pit that measures nine feet by seven feet. A pile of mine tailings is next to this pit.

The 1910 Geological Survey of New Jersey states that this mine was opened in 1872 and that the ore body was twelve feet wide. The mine is described as a "shallow trench and a few holes" on the east slope of the mountain. The surface evidence of a shallow pit and few rock tailings clearly indicate that this mine was purely exploratory in nature.

Rockaway Valley Mines

*T*he Rockaway Valley Mines (figure 33), also known as the DeCamp Mines, are a complex of shafts, trenches, large open pits, exploratory pits, roads and work staging areas located on the western slope of Stony Brook Mountain in Montville and Boonton Townships, Morris County, New Jersey. The mine complex is a short distance to the west and southwest of the Decker Mine previously described and can be reached by following the same road. From the Decker Mine, follow the old road up the mountain to where the terrain levels out. A large split-rock boulder is situated to the left of the road on the mountaintop. Turn left here and follow the old road in a southwesterly direction. The mine openings and other features will be seen along the steep hillside to the left of the road.

The first major opening encountered along the old road is an open trench which has been cut into the rocky hillside near the road. This open cut is twenty-eight feet long, five feet wide and six feet deep at its maximum. A large pile of mine tailings is present adjacent to the trench. From this opening, additional mine shafts can be seen up the steep hillside at some distance from the road.

A mine shaft which slopes at a forty-five degree angle into the hillside is located about fifty feet to the east and above the level of the road. This shaft extends fifteen feet into the rock, is eight feet wide and about fifteen feet deep. It is filled with water and is dangerous. The opening faces southwest, and there is a tailing pile in front of the shaft or downslope. Another vertical shaft is located a short distance to the south along the same steep hillside. This vertical shaft measures ten feet by eight feet by ten feet deep. It is filled with leaves and is situated about 300 feet to the east of the road and about 100 feet above the road. There is a large pile of tailings on the downslope side of the shaft.

Two large, contiguous open pits are located on the

hillside to the east of the road. The location of these features can easily be determined by hiking along the road. The first noticeable features to be seen are two long trenches, probably used for drainage, which came down the hillside from the area of the open pits. Also, there is a stone retaining wall and a flat work or staging area, twenty-two feet by twelve feet, along the easterly side of the road just below the mine openings. At this point, climb up the steep hillside to the mine openings. The northerly pit is seventy-five feet long, thirty-five feet wide and about twenty feet deep. The southerly pit is thirty-one feet long, twenty-three feet wide and fifteen feet deep. There is a very large tailings pile on the downslope side of these large pits.

There are two vertical shafts and one slanting trench located higher up the steep hillside near the open pits described above. The first shaft is ten feet by eight feet and extends at an angle into the rock hillside to a depth of twenty feet. Tailings are piled adjacent to the shaft, and a short road connects this shaft with the two open pits below. The second vertical shaft is located about sixty feet to the south of the one just described and near the top of the hill. It is ten feet by eight feet by five feet deep, filled with water, and has a small tailings pile next to it. Moving southerly along the steep hillside, hikers will encounter a trench. This trench is twenty-four feet long, ten feet wide and six feet deep, and it is filled with water. It has been cut into the mountain on an angle, with rock debris or tailings on the downhill side of the long trench. Again, a small road extends down the hillside from this mine cut and can be followed by the alert hiker.

The Rockaway Valley Mines were first explored in 1820 but apparently not worked to any extent. In 1870, five openings were excavated, and in 1872 two additional shafts were sunk. The northeastern ore body was worked by William S. DeCamp until 1873, when it was shut down as a result of poor economic conditions nationwide. The ore was shipped to the Musconetcong

Ironworks at Stanhope, New Jersey, via the Morris Canal. The mines were reopened again in 1879, worked for a short time, and finally shut down and abandoned in 1880.

In 1872, a new method of transmitting power was employed at the mines. The hoisting of men and ore and the pumping of air and the removal of water was carried out by a single steam engine. The power was transmitted by wire rope which ran over friction wheels; a series of clutches connected or disconnected the loads as necessary.

The two southwest mine shafts opened in 1872 produced 500 tons of ore. The five pits opened in 1870 were producing 450 tons of ore per month in 1872. In the period beginning with the fall of 1879 to 1880, 500 tons of ore were raised from the Rockaway Valley Mines.

Figure 34: Drawing of trench at Surebridge Mine. Notches are cut into the vertical side walls to hold supporting timbers.

Iron Mines and Trails in New York

Black Ash Mine

*T*he Trail Conference Harriman Trails Map #3 shows two mine openings along the Ramapo-Dunderberg Trail in the Town of Tuxedo, Orange County, New York. These mine openings are situated south of Black Ash Brook, about 1.5 miles from the beginning of the Ramapo-Dunderberg Trail at the Tuxedo railroad station (figure 35). They were dug along a steeply sloping hillside and are at an elevation of approximately 900 feet above mean sea level. (On the 1995 edition of the Harriman map, these mine openings are not shown correctly; they are actually located about 0.3 mile farther north along the trail.)

To reach the Black Ash Mine, park at the Tuxedo railroad station (hiker parking is permitted here only on weekends and holidays) and follow the Ramapo-Dunderberg (R-D) Trail (red-dot-on-white blazes), which begins at the station platform. The trail goes south along the tracks for about 500 feet, then turns left and crosses the Ramapo River on a footbridge. After going under the Thruway, the R-D Trail turns left on Grove Drive. About half a mile from the start, the trail turns right and enters the woods. In another half a mile, there is a beautiful viewpoint to the left over the village of Tuxedo.

Soon afterwards, the R-D Trail bears right and continues along an old woods road which comes up from below. This road once provided access to the Black Ash Mine. In another 300 feet, the Tuxedo-Mt. Ivy Trail (red-dash-on-white blazes) begins to the right. Continue straight

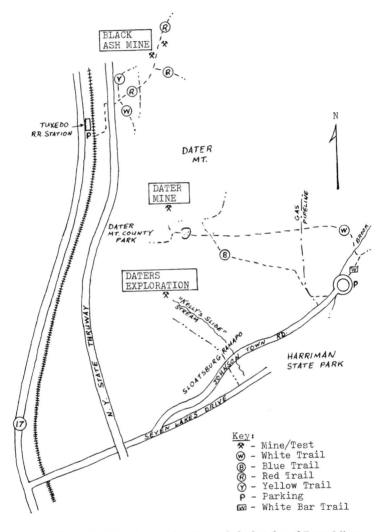

Figure 35: Map showing locations of Black Ash and Dater Mines, and Dater's Exploration.

ahead on the R-D Trail, and in another 0.25 mile you will reach the first mine opening, to the left of the trail. This mine opening is only sixteen feet from the trail, and a large pile of tailings indicates its location. The second mine opening is about 500 feet north of the first opening. It is about 150 feet to the right of the trail on the steep hillside and, again, its adjacent pile of tailings is visible from the trail.

The first mine opening is a slanting shaft which measures thirteen feet by eleven feet; it is usually filled with water and is about ten feet deep toward its south end. A large tailings pile is present at the north side of the shaft, which suggests that considerable effort was expended in extracting ore from this shaft. There are two shallow exploratory pits located nearby.

The second mine opening is a vertical shaft which measures twenty feet in length from east to west and thirteen feet in width from north to south. This shaft is also filled with water and is eleven feet deep at its easterly side. A large pile of tailings is present on the west side of the shaft, and this feature suggests extensive exploration effort for iron ore.

An abandoned woods road is located about 0.3 mile south of the Black Ash Mine; it comes up the steep hillside and extends past the mine

---

The Black Ash Mine consists of one slanting shaft, and one vertical shaft

---

openings, connecting with the Black Ash Swamp Road on the north. These woods roads provided access to the mine.

The history of the Black Ash Mine is not known. The mine openings are not indicated on earlier versions of the trail maps, probably because this area was private land until the 1950s. Trail historian William Myles speculates that "the ore must have gone to Solomon Townsend's Augusta Works at Tuxedo, about 1800." However, this is unlikely, as the mine openings appear to be of more recent origin. Perhaps they are associated with the Greenwood group of mines which were discovered and opened around 1880 and which provided iron ore to the blast furnaces at Arden, New York.

Dater Mine

*H*igh atop Dater Mountain at an elevation of 920 feet above mean sea level is a large open pit known as the Dater Mine (figure 35). The mine is located in Harriman State Park, just north of Dater Mountain Nature County Park in the Town of Ramapo, Rockland County, New York. The site is northeast of the Village of Sloatsburg.

To reach the mine, park at the end of Johnsontown Road and take the Blue Disc Trail, heading in a northwesterly direction. After 0.45 mile, the white-blazed Kakiat Trail briefly joins, and then goes off to the left. Continue on the Kakiat Trail for about 700 feet beyond the junction, to where the trail makes a sharp bend to the left. Here, an old woods road goes off to the right. Follow this old road, which ascends the mountain rather steeply. After climbing about 120 feet, the old road bends sharply to the right. At this point (elevation 760 feet), abandon the road and continue climbing up to the top of the mountain, where the mine will be readily apparent. Two hemlock trees are growing in front of it.

The Dater Mine is a large open cut, fifty feet in length by thirty-five feet in width. At the northern end of this cut, the mine extends into the mountainside for an additional fifteen feet and appears to slant downward. This section is filled with water and is dangerous. A pillar of

> **The Dater Mine consists of a large open pit located high atop Dater Mountain**

rock in the middle of the mine entrance supports the roof of the mine. At the south end of the open cut is a flat terrace constructed of mine tailings that have been dumped along the edge of the mountain. This terrace affords a scenic vista of the surrounding area (in the summer, the view may be obscured by the foliage).

The remains of an unidentified structure are present on top of the mountain about fifty feet to the north of the mine. This feature appears to be a stone foundation or cellar hole, now filled in, that measures thirteen feet by twelve feet. The size of this feature and its below-ground construction suggest that it may have been a powder magazine or storage area for the nearby mine.

An abandoned mine road decends from the mine and summit along the westerly side of the mountain and heads in a northerly direction. To find this road, stand a few feet from the edge of the terrace, facing the center of the mine. Turn left in a west-northwesterly direction (about 290 degrees). You will see the road along the edge of the hilltop. Follow this road northwesterly along the brow of the hill for about 90 feet. You will note the presence of iron ore which has been deposited along the outer or left side of the road. At this point, the road turns and descends from the mountaintop in a northerly direction. As you proceed down the road, you will observe that the sides of the road are lined with stones — large cobbles — which delineate its route. Soon the road reaches a small plateau. Here, it becomes more obscure and difficult to follow. Eventually, you will come to another road which descends steeply to the left. This road will lead down to the Kakiat Trail. Or, if you wish, you can bushwhack down the hillside to the Kakiat Trail.

Unfortunately, little is known about the history of the Dater Mine. It was probably associated with Abraham Dater, who operated two iron forges on the Ramapo River and one on Stony Brook in the first half of the nineteenth century. Dater also owned 2,600 acres of land in the area between the Ramapo River and Stony Brook.

Dater's Exploration

Extensive evidence of iron mining activity may be found near the top of a hill located just to the north of the Village of Sloatsburg-Town of Ramapo boundary line. There are two horizontal mine shafts near the bottom of a westerly facing cliff or ridge at an elevation of about 640 feet above mean sea level. This mine site (figure 35), known as Dater's Exploration, is on private land about 930 feet northwest of Johnsontown Road and can be reached by following a stream up to the

The origins of Dater's Exploration are lost to history

top of the rise. Since the mine is on private property, permission should be obtained from the owner to hike to the site. To reach the mine site, park at the cul-de-sac at the end of Johnsontown Road and walk southwest along the road for 0.8 mile until you reach a small stream which comes down the mountain, flows under the road, and enters Stony Brook. (Just before reaching this stream, the stone abutments of a bridge which once crossed Stony Brook are visible to the southeast of the road.)

Turn right and continue uphill in a northwesterly direction, following along the right side of the stream. The ravine through which the stream flows is narrow, with steep rock sides. An old Harriman Park Trail Guide refers to this V-shaped rocky channel as "Kelly's Slide." The mine shafts are in the side of a cliff to the right (northeast) of the ravine, a short distance beyond the crest of the rise of the ravine. They are about 40 feet higher than the crest of the ravine, and about 250 feet northeast of it.

The northernmost mine shaft slopes downward into the hillside. It is twenty feet long, eight feet wide and five and one-half feet high, but the entrance is only about three feet high. A drill mark is visible on the roof of the mine just beyond the entrance. The second mine shaft is located a short distance to the south and slightly higher on the hillside. It is thirty-six feet deep, six feet wide and six and one-half feet high, and the far end of the shaft contains water. A third mine working is also present along the ridge to the south and consists of an open cut or trench twenty feet in length and nine and one-half feet in height. This latter mine cut may have extended horizontally into the cliff itself, but it appears to have been filled in. There are large piles of ore or tailings near the entrance to each mine shaft.

The history of this iron mine is obscure. Rockland County historian Arthur Tompkins stated in 1902 that "no iron ore... was mined or produced within the Town of Ramapo." However, the existence of these workings, as well as the Dater Mine located less than a mile to the north, clearly contradict this statement. Although no documentary evidence has been found regarding the history of these horizontal shafts, they were probably associated with the Dater Mine activity and date to the 19th century.

Boston Mine

*T*he Boston Mine (figure 36) is situated within a belt of magnetite which is referred to as the Greenwood group of mines. It is located on the Dunning Trail in Harriman State Park, about three-quarters of a mile north of Route 106 and a short distance to the east of an old woods road known as the Island Pond Road.

To reach the Boston Mine, hikers should leave their cars in a parking area on the south side of Route 106, a short distance east of the White Bar Trail crossing.

According to historian James M. Ransom the Boston Mine was worked around 1880

Walk back along the road to the White Bar Trail, and follow the trail north for about 300 feet to a fork. Bear left at the fork (leaving the white-blazed trail) and continue north along the woods road. After about three-quarters of a mile, the white-blazed Nurian Trail briefly joins the road, and soon afterwards the yellow-blazed Dunning Trail joins from the left. In another 400 feet, turn right as the Dunning Trail leaves the woods road, and follow the Dunning Trail for about 150 feet. Where the trail turns right and uphill, continue straight ahead and enter the mine.

The mine opening consists of a large open cut,

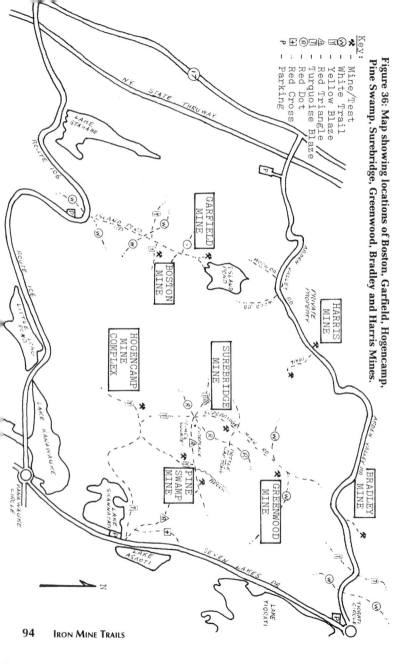

Figure 36: Map showing locations of Boston, Garfield, Hogencamp, Pine Swamp, Surebridge, Greenwood, Bradley and Harris Mines.

Key:
- ⚒ — Mine/Test
- Ⓦ — White Trail
- Ⓨ — Yellow Blaze
- △ — Red Triangle
- ▯ — Turquoise Blaze
- Ⓡ — Red Dot
- ⊞ — Red Cross
- P — Parking

about 100 feet long, which extends north to south within a low ridge. At its northern end, the open cut becomes a shaft which extends into the rock ridge for about 30 feet. One can enter the open cut by means of an entrance near its southwestern side, but the northern end and shaft are water-filled and dangerous.

A trip to the Garfield Mine will reward both hikers and mine enthusiasts

---

An ore dump is present near the entrance to the mine.

The remains of the mine's work and staging area can be seen along the Island Pond Road, just south of its junction with the Dunning Trail. This area is generally flat and was cleared of trees at one time. There is a stone foundation in this location.

According to historian James M. Ransom, the Boston Mine was worked around 1880. The ore extracted from this mine was sent to the Clove Furnace at Arden, New York to be smelted.

Garfield Mine

*T*his mine, located at the south end of Island Pond in Harriman State Park, has been repeatedly described by historians as being "submerged in swamps" or that "the shaft is filled with water." These reports suggest that the mine no longer exists; consequently, its location is not shown on trail maps of the park, nor is it described in recent guidebooks. However, evidence of the Garfield Mine does exist on the landscape, and a trip to this site will be a rewarding one for hikers and mine enthusiasts alike.

The Garfield Mine (figure 36) can be easily reached by hiking the Island Pond Road north from Route 106. Hikers should park in the parking area just east of the White Bar Trail crossing and follow the woods road to the north (see directions above for Boston Mine). Continue past the intersections with the white-blazed Nurian Trail and the yellow-blazed Dunning Trail. About 1.1 miles from Route 106, the red-triangle-on-white-blazed Arden-

Surebridge (A-SB) Trail comes in from the right. Just beyond this point, there is a fork in the road. Bear right (the A-SB Trail goes left here) and continue for another 0.2 mile. Here, there is another fork in the road. Bear left and continue walking for about

---

The remains of the Garfield Mine consist of two exploratory pits and an open trench

---

250 feet. The Garfield Mine is located at the end of the left fork of the road, on the right (east) side of the road.

The remains of the Garfield Mine consist of two exploratory pits and a large open trench. The first feature which the hiker will encounter is an oval exploratory pit, which measures twelve feet in length from north to south and ten feet from east to west. About five feet north of this exploratory pit is the large open trench. This trench, which is surrounded by mountain laurel, is keyhole in shape. It is fifty-eight feet long, twenty-six feet wide at its northern end and ten feet wide along its southern

section. A drainage ditch is present at the northwest side of the trench. The trench is filled with water; thus, its original depth has not been determined. However, the depth from ground level to the water level on the east side of the trench is five feet. A second exploratory pit is located about fifteen feet west of the large open trench. It is circular and measures ten feet in diameter. Piles of mine tailings are present in the vicinity of these openings.

In addition to mountain laurel, there are a number of hemlock trees in the immediate area of the mine. A large white pine tree is another natural feature at the site.

Little is known about the extent and operation of the Garfield Mine. The mine was owned by Robert and Peter Parrott, and it supplied iron ore to the Clove and Greenwood furnaces at Arden, New York. The mine was reportedly abandoned by 1880.

After visiting the Garfield Mine, hikers may wish to continue to Island Pond. To reach the pond, return to the last fork in Island Pond Road and turn left. This branch of the road leads to the ruins of a stone cabin on a point of land overlooking the pond.

Island Pond is a natural body of water, situated in a large glacially-made pothole, that drains both north and south. In the early twentieth century, a dam was built at the northern end of the pond which raised the water level three to four feet. The deepest part of the pond is 126 feet, with depths averaging ninety-one feet in the northern half. Island Pond — with its rocky shore on the north, an island off its east shore, and swamps at its south end — is unsurpassed in its scenic beauty.

Hogencamp Mine

*T*he Hogencamp Mine (figure 36) is an extensive mining complex situated in the rugged mountains of Harriman State Park about one-half mile north of Route 106. Black Rock Mountain lies southwest of the mine and Hogencamp Mountain lies to the northwest. The Hogencamp Mine is part of the Greenwood group of mines, which furnished ore to the blast furnace at Arden, New York. The mine complex can easily be reached by taking the turquoise-blazed Long Path from the parking area at Lake Skannatati and following it west for 1.3 miles to its junction with the yellow-blazed Dunning Trail. Take the Dunning Trail, an old mine road, south for about 500 feet to the mine complex. The Dunning Trail runs through the complex; the Long Path runs above and north of the complex. There are six open pits, trenches and shafts within this mine complex, and the area also contains the remains of a number of structures which were part of the complex (figure 37).

The ruins of several structures can be seen on both sides of the Dunning Trail at the northeastern end of the complex. On the northwest side of the road are the remains of three structures: A U-shaped stone foundation, twenty-six feet by twenty feet, with walls three feet thick; a possible banked powder magazine, sixteen feet by ten feet, with walls three and one-half feet thick; and a dry-laid stone foundation, ten feet by ten feet, with a large boulder

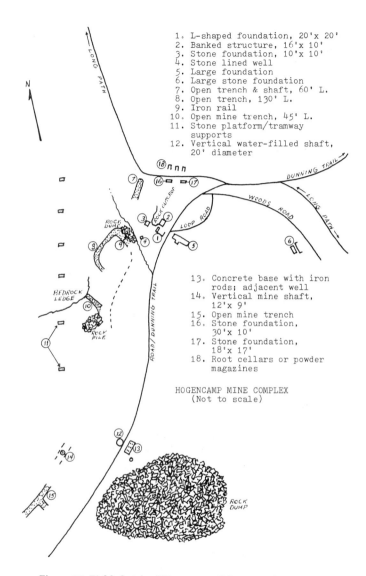

1. L-shaped foundation, 20'x 20'
2. Banked structure, 16'x 10'
3. Stone foundation, 10'x 10'
4. Stone lined well
5. Large foundation
6. Large stone foundation
7. Open trench & shaft, 60' L.
8. Open trench, 130' L.
9. Iron rail
10. Open mine trench, 45' L.
11. Stone platform/tramway supports
12. Vertical water-filled shaft, 20' diameter

13. Concrete base with iron rods; adjacent well
14. Vertical mine shaft, 12'x 9'
15. Open mine trench
16. Stone foundation, 30'x 10'
17. Stone foundation, 18'x 17'
18. Root cellars or powder magazines

HOGENCAMP MINE COMPLEX
(Not to scale)

Figure 37: Field sketch of Hogencamp Mine complex, 1995.

forming part of the foundation on its south side. To the south of these structures is a stone-lined well, five feet in diameter.

Other structural ruins may be found on the southeast side of the Dunning Trail, opposite the features just described. Adjacent to the road is a large stone foundation. This structure has three bays and a partial cellar hole. It is of dry-stone construction and may be the remains of a barn or possibly the saloon and dance hall which reportedly existed at this mine complex. A narrow wagon road extends from the northeast end of the structure and goes up the hill where it turns, makes a loop, and joins another woods road. This woods road begins at the Dunning Trail about seventy-five feet west of its intersection with the Long Path and proceeds south. The first part of this road is overgrown with mountain laurel, but it soon opens up and becomes clearly recognizable as a road. Travel about 250 feet down this road, and you will notice a stone foundation on the right (west) side, some thirty feet from the road. This structural ruin is at the edge of the hillside and overlooks a swamp. It is constructed of cut stone laid up dry and measures twenty-six feet by twenty-two feet. A partial

The Hogencamp Mine is an extensive complex in the rugged mountains of Harriman State Park

cellar hole is visible at the north end of the foundation, and a flat U-shaped stone foundation is four feet to the east.

The most impressive mine shaft is at the northeastern end of the complex, immediately adjacent to and just below the Long Path. Here, there is an open trench about six feet in width and forty feet in length, extending an additional twenty feet into the rocky hillside as a horizontal shaft. The bottom of this shaft is filled with water. A short distance to the west is another open shaft somewhat U-shaped in layout that is 130 feet in length and ten feet wide. Within the easternmost leg of this trench is a single piece of narrow gauge iron rail, eight and one-half feet long, with one end buried in the ground. This iron rail suggests the location of track on which skip cars ran, carrying the ore out of the large open mine cut.

To the southwest of the large U-shaped trench is

The most impressive mine shaft is at the northeastern edge of the Hogencamp complex

---

another open mine trench. This trench is forty-five feet long and terminates in a water-filled pit, eight feet wide, at the base of a bedrock ledge. There is a rock pile adjacent to the open end of the trench.

A short distance further west along the sloping hillside are two stone platforms that once served as supports for a tramway which hauled ore in buckets up and across the mountain top. The tramway consisted of a steel cable suspended above the ground, extending from the mine north-northeasterly for about half a mile to a terminus on the mountaintop where the ore buckets were unloaded. The steel cable

passed over cast-iron pulleys as it moved the ore buckets; power for the cable was supplied by a steam engine located at its northern terminus. Four more stone tramway supports may be found on top of the mountain immediately adjacent to the mine. The line of these stone bases can be followed up and along the mountain, crossing the Long Path and continuing through a narrow ravine to the terminus of the tramway, again on the Long Path. The foundation of the cable house and other structural ruins may be seen at the northern end of the tramway adjacent to the Long Path.

Two vertical shafts are present on the northwest side of the road south of the lower tramway supports. Both vertical shafts are dangerous and should be approached and observed with extreme caution. The first shaft, located at the edge of the road, measures twenty-five feet in diameter and is filled with water. A cast-iron pipe, six and three-quarter inches in diameter, extends vertically from the water-filled shaft; it was once used to dewater the mine.

Adjacent to the mine shaft is an iron rod with a bolt at its end.

On the southeast side of the road, opposite this water-filled shaft, are the remains of a concrete machinery mount with iron rods. These features anchored the steam engine which produced power for the drilling, hoisting and dewatering operations in the nearby mine cuts. A stone-lined well, three feet in diameter, is situated nearby and probably supplied the water for the engine. An

> *In 1880, men working day and night shifts removed 11,500 tons of ore from the mine*

extensive rock and tailing dump is present in the surrounding area.

A second vertical mine shaft is located southwest of the first shaft and seventy-seven feet northwest of the road. It is rectangular, about twelve feet by nine feet. At the far western end of the complex is still another open trench, 150 feet in length and ten feet wide, running along the rocky hillside.

The remains of several former mine structures are present along the Long Path just to the northwest of the mining complex. This area was part of a little village that once flourished adjacent to the mine. Historian James M. Ransom states that some twenty houses, several barns, a school and a store were once located in this general area.

On the west side of the Long Path are two stone foundations. One is thirty feet by ten feet with a center partition wall, while the second is a dry-laid cut stone foundation which measures eighteen feet by seventeen feet. The presence of artifacts on the surface of the ground in the vicinity of these structures, such as coal, glass and ceramic fragments and an iron water pipe, suggests that they may be the remains of domestic buildings. Three banked ruins, U-shaped, are visible on the east side of the Long Path and may be the remains of root cellars or powder storage magazines.

Iron ore was mined at this site from 1870 to 1885. The ore vein was twelve to fifteen feet in width. In 1880,

11,500 tons of ore were mined at the site, and by that time the ore vein had been worked to a depth of sixty feet and a length of 250 feet. Oral history tells us that the Hogencamp Mine operated on a two-shift schedule: four gangs of men dug ore on the day shift and three gangs of men worked at night. Other men loaded the skip cars which were pulled by mules or horses.

Pine Swamp Mine

*T*he Pine Swamp Mine (figure 36), among the most dramatic old mining complexes in Harriman State Park, gets its name from the adjacent wetland. It consists of a complex of features, including open cuts, pits, shafts, and the ruins of homes, barns and powder storage magazines. This mine complex is located in the area surrounding the junction of the Arden-Surebridge (A-SB) Trail and the Dunning Trail in Harriman State Park. The site is about three-fourths of a mile northwest of the Lake Skannatati parking area and can be reached by taking the Arden-Surebridge Trail (red-triangle-on-white blazes) for 1.25 miles to its junction with the Dunning Trail (yellow blazes). The Pine Swamp Mine can also be reached from the Hogencamp Mine by following the Dunning Trail to the north-east for about three-quarters of a mile.

The largest and most spectacular opening in this complex is located on the hillside above the Dunning Trail, about 900 feet south of its intersection with the A-SB Trail. A large mine dump of rock or tailings rises about fifty feet on the northwest side of the trail, and the workings are up the hillside nearby. This mine is a large open cut about 100 feet long and forty feet wide, with vertical walls seventy-five feet high. Drill holes are visible on the rock walls, along with square and horizontal notches. The notches were probably seats for timber bracing. A rectangular water-filled shaft containing the remains of timbers is located along the bottom of the west wall of the open cut. At the southern end of the cut is an adit or opening to a horizontal passage that extends some 125 feet into the hillside. This passage slopes upward, and above its far end is an air shaft opening to the surface. On a sunny day, light pours through this rock-bound skylight, illuminating the long passage.

There are at least two other mine workings located along the hillside, just west of the Dunning Trail. To find these openings (after visiting the main opening described above), the hiker should go north along the hillside, parallel to the Dunning Trail. The first opening is a shaft, fifteen feet by fifteen feet, which is presently filled with water. The second mine opening — on the hillside, about 200 feet north of the first opening and about 500 feet south of the intersection with the A-SB Trail — is an open cut, twenty-eight feet long and ten feet wide, with vertical side walls twelve feet deep. A small stream and waterfall flows past the entrance to this cut and empties into the nearby swamp. There appears to have been a shaft, now filled in, near the entrance.

A number of mine openings may be found along the nearby Arden-Surebridge Trail, which also follows the route of an old mine road. The most prominent of these

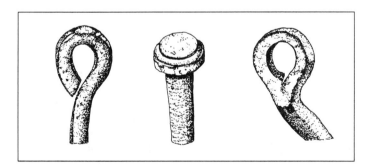

Figure 38: Drawing of hand-forged iron tie rods found at Pine Swamp Mine (specimen at left) and Surebridge Mine.

is about 100 feet east of the A-SB/Dunning intersection. It is a large rectangular cut on a low hilltop that is 118 feet long and twenty-nine feet wide, with vertical rock walls that are about twenty-two feet deep. This open cut is presently filled with water. About 200 feet farther east along the trail is another large open trench, fifty-five feet long and eleven feet wide, which contains several drilling holes. Two water-filled shafts — one thirty feet by sixteen feet, with a stone retaining wall at one end, and the other ten and one-half

---

The Pine Swamp Mine's most spectacular opening is on the hillside above the Dunning Trail

---

feet by ten and one-half feet — are on the north side of the road just east of the trenches, while a test pit and large piles of tailings may be seen on the south side of the road.

The remains of several structures may be seen farther east along the Arden-Surebridge Trail. On the east side of Pine Swamp, about 500 feet southeast from where the A-SB Trail leaves the old mine road, are the ruins of a dwelling foundation measuring twenty-one feet four inches by eighteen feet three inches, with an interior stone pile which is a collapsed fireplace and chimney. Nearby are two semi-subterranean dry-stone foundations, one nine feet eight inches by six feet three inches, and the other twelve feet by twelve feet, which were probably powder storage magazines or root cellars. Just to the northwest of these structures there is a stone retaining wall.

About 300 feet west of the junction of the A-SB and Dunning Trails, the remains of a stone dwelling foundation and two storage cellars with earth-banked walls may be seen. These features are on the north side of the road (now the A-SB Trail), about fifty feet from the road. The dwelling foundation measures thirty-eight feet in length by eighteen feet in width and has a center dividing wall. The two storage cellars have dry-laid stone interiors.

The Pine Swamp Mine, part of the Greenwood group

of mines, was opened around 1830 and worked intermittently until 1880. The mine was owned by Robert and Peter Parrott, and the ore was brought to their smelting furnaces at Arden, New York.

Surebridge Mine

*T*he Surebridge Mine (figure 36) is located on the east side of the Surebridge Mine Road, about one-half mile north of the "Times Square" junction of the Arden-Surebridge, Ramapo-Dunderberg, and Long Path Trails. A brook and swamp are located to the west and southwest of the mine complex.

To reach the Surebridge Mine, leave your car at the parking area at Lake Skannatati, and proceed west either on the red-triangle-on-white-blazed Arden-Surebridge (A-SB) Trail, or on the turquoise-blazed Long Path, to Times Square. The distance via the A-SB Trail is 1.7 miles; it is 2.1 miles via the Long Path. From Times Square, continue north on the joint A-SB/Long Path for about 500 feet, until these

trails turn left, leaving the old woods road that they have been following. Continue north along this road, known as the Surebridge Mine Road, passing the Surebridge Swamp to the left. In another 0.4 mile — just beyond the northern end of the swamp — you will see the mine to the right of the road.

There are eight mine openings within this complex. Nearest the road is a small test pit. Behind it is an oval-shaped trench or cut, sixty feet by twenty feet, which is also filled with water. In back of that is a rectangular water-filled cut that measures twelve feet by ten feet.

Further back and to the east of the road are several other mine features. There are three open cuts or trenches on a flat terrace. The southernmost trench is eighty feet long and twenty feet wide, with notches cut into the vertical side walls (figure 34). These notches were seats for timbers used in bracing the side walls. Two narrow open cuts, each about eighty feet long, lie parallel to each other at the north end of the site. Two iron tie rods are near the south end of the easterly trench, and a third is just beyond the south end of the westerly trench (figure 38).

A water-filled hole, eight feet by eight feet, with laid-up stone work on two sides, is located sixteen feet south of the western trench. It appears to be enclosed within a flat work-staging area, with a low semi-circular stone retaining wall visible on the west and south sides of the work area. A deep vertical shaft, with a twelve-foot-by-eight-foot opening, is located thirty-nine feet south of the small hole just described. In the winter of 1995, this vertical shaft was filled with water to sixteen feet below ground level. This shaft is precipitous and difficult to look into without a sense of vertigo; some of its edges are undercut and could slump with extra weight. It should be approached and viewed with extreme caution.

A stone platform, ten feet by seven feet in size, is located twenty-six feet to the east of the north end of the eighty-foot-by-twenty-foot trench. It is constructed of large rectangular cut-stone blocks; a vertical iron rod is embedded in one of these stones. A drainage ditch extends along the east side of the long trench, and the stone platform may have been the seat for the dewatering equipment used to pump out the water from the adjacent trench.

Finally, the ruins of a banked stone structure with a stone-lined interior which measures fourteen feet by thirteen feet are visible to the east and slightly upslope of the narrow eighty-foot-long easterly trench. This banked structure has a keyhole entrance that is ten feet long

---

At the Surebridge Mine, note the notches cut into the rock as seats to hold timber braces

---

and two feet wide. The structure was, most likely, a powder storage magazine. Tailing piles and other small test pits are also present at the site.

According to historian James M. Ransom, the Surebridge Mine was owned and operated by Robert and Peter Parrott in the 19th century. The mine was particularly active during the Civil War, and the ore was sent to the Greenwood Furnace at Arden, New York, for smelting. In 1880, records indicate that 458 tons of iron ore were extracted from the mine.

Greenwood Mine

*T*he Greenwood Mine (figure 36) is located near the junction of the Appalachian Trail and the Surebridge Mine Road in Harriman State Park. The site can be easily reached by parking at Lake Skannatati and taking the red-triangle-on-white-blazed Arden-Surebridge (A-SB) Trail or the turquoise-blazed Long Path to Times Square. From Times Square, continue north on the joint A-SB/Long Path for about 500 feet. When these trails turn left and leave the road they have been following, continue north along the road, known as the Surebridge Mine Road, for about a mile, until the white-blazed Appalachian Trail joins from the left. The Greenwood Mine is on the right side of the road, just beyond this point. (Alterna-

tively, you can park at the Tiorati Circle, walk up Arden Valley Road in a westerly direction for 0.3 mile until the Appalachian Trail crosses, then proceed south on the Appalachian Trail. The trail runs along the ridge of Fingerboard Mountain for about a mile, then turns right and begins to descend. At the base of a steep descent, about 1.6 miles from Arden Valley Road, the trail turns left and joins the Surebridge Mine Road. The mine is on the left side of the trail, a short distance beyond this point.)

The physical remains of the Greenwood Mine suggest that this operation was extensive and activity spanned a long period of time. A large open pit, 100 feet long by thirty feet wide, now filled with water, is located on the east side of the old road. Near the north end of this pit is a brick platform containing vertical iron rods, which probably functioned as a base for a steam engine. Lying on the surface nearby is a length of iron pipe, twelve feet two inches long and twelve inches in diameter. A short distance to the south-east of the open pit is another irregular open trench 100 feet in length. Large tailing piles are present along the stream near the west side of the road.

Several exploratory pits, a vertical shaft and a horizontal shaft, all filled with water, may be seen along the hillside to the east of the road. A platform constructed of rough cut stone and measuring fifteen feet by fifteen feet can be observed in this area.

The Greenwood Mine, also known as the Patterson Mine, was first opened in 1838. The ore from this mine

---

The Greenwood Mine supplied iron ore to local furnaces during the Civil War

---

has been described as hard, compact, and containing iron pyrites which required roasting prior to being smelted in a blast furnace. The mine was owned by Robert and Peter Parrott and supplied ore to the Clove and Greenwood furnaces at Arden, New York, during the Civil War. The Greenwood Mine was last worked in 1880.

Bradley Mine

This mine is stunning. A long open trench leading to the shaft in the hillside lends an air of mystery and excitement to the site. In the wintertime, the large mine chamber — with stalagmites and stalactites, formed by dripping ground water — overpowers the viewing hiker. Huge icicles are formed at the entrance to the chamber, and their spectacular beauty is a photographer's delight.

The Bradley Mine (figure 36) is located in Harriman State Park on the north side of Arden Valley Road about 0.9 mile west of the Tiorati Circle (and 0.3 mile west of the Long Path crossing). An old road, 400 feet in length, rises steeply up the hillside heading in a northeasterly direction to the mine entrance. The mine consists of an open cut on the hillside that is about 200 feet long and nearly fifty feet deep near its northerly end. At the north end of the open cut there is a shaft or chamber that extends into the rock hillside. The chamber is cavernous — about fifty feet wide and twenty feet high — and it extends at least 100 feet into the hillside. It is filled with water. This chamber reportedly once contained a rich pocket of ore. An opening, probably an air shaft, is located along the roof of the chamber on its southerly side. Several drill marks can be seen along the walls of the open cut and within the chamber itself. This mine must be approached and viewed with extreme caution.

The old mine road extends further up the hillside for an additional 350 feet to the top of the mine entrance. A spectacular view of the mine chamber from above awaits the hiker. Two large tailing piles or mine dumps are present on the hilltop, just south of the mine entrance.

Several structural and landscape features are present along the north side of Arden Valley Road just below the mine. The remains of a banked structure, with an interior stone-lined chamber measuring eight feet by four feet, are visible southeast of the mine, about seventy-five feet north of Arden Valley Road. This structure probably once functioned as a powder storage area. To the west of this powder magazine, and up the hillside, is a flat work-staging area extending over 875 square feet.

The Bradley Mine was operated extensively during the Civil War, and its ore was shipped to the Clove and Greenwood furnaces at

---

A long open trench leading to a hillside shaft lends an air of mystery to the Bradley Mine

---

Arden, New York. During this period, it was owned and operated by Robert and Peter Parrott. The mine ceased operating in 1874.

Trail historian William J. Myles indicates that the mine was named for a man named Bradley who "opened iron mines on the land" sometime during the Revolutionary War. No further information is presently available about this person. Perhaps he was related to Richard Bradley, who was appointed Attorney-General for the Colony of New York in 1722. Bradley and his children received several large grants of land in the Highlands region from King George II, including the "Richard Bradley Bear Hill Tract" (now part of Bear Mountain State Park) and other tracts in the area. Bradley died in 1749.

Harris Mine

*F*or many years, the location of the Harris Mine (figure 36) in Harriman State Park has been shrouded in mystery. Older (pre-1995) editions of the New York-New Jersey Trail Conference Harriman maps show the mine as being located southeast of Arden Valley Road. Its location is indicated on the south slope of Echo Mountain at an elevation of approximately 1,100 feet above mean sea level and near a wetland. These older Trail Conference maps also show two unmarked trails leading to the mine, one heading southeasterly from Arden Valley Road and the other extending southwesterly from the road leading to Upper Lake Cohasset. These two "unmarked trails" are in reality well-constructed former roads, now long abandoned and rather difficult to follow. An exploratory pit, fifteen feet by thirteen feet and two and one-half feet deep, is located near the end of the old road which comes up from Arden Valley Road. Evidence of logging operations and other shallow exploratory pits may be seen along the old road that comes up the mountain from the road to Upper Lake Cohasset. Along this easterly road is a large beech tree. Carved into its trunk are the words "cut off 1909," indicating that this area was once a wood lot which was harvested in that year.

The exploratory pits, roads, and other features described above are not, however, the main complex of the Harris Mine. The Harris Mine is located on the northwest side of Arden Valley Road, 0.6 mile northeast of the road which leads to Island Pond (this road ends at a gate on the south side of Arden Valley Road). Coming from the west, the mine is situated on the left side of Arden Valley Road, just before the road begins a steady descent. It is directly opposite an abandoned road which is visible on the hillside on the southeast side of Arden Valley Road. The mine openings are less than 100 feet from Arden Valley Road on private land which

---

The Harris Mine consists of two large workings: a vertical shaft and a long trench

---

is closed to the public. It is clear to the keen observer that the now-abandoned road once extended from the Harris Mine in a southeasterly direction up Echo Mountain, but was cut by the construction of the present Arden Valley Road, which occurred in the 1930s. The original Arden Valley Road is located to the north, within the private estate, and extends from the Clove and Greenwood furnaces at Arden, New York, easterly towards the Tiorati Circle.

The Harris Mine consists of two large workings: the first is a vertical oval-shaped shaft, nineteen feet by fifteen feet by five feet deep, which is filled with water. A small pile of tailings lies nearby. The second opening is located fifty-eight feet to the south of the vertical shaft. It is an open cut or trench that is twenty-eight feet long and eight feet wide. At its easterly end, the trench is nine feet deep, filled with water, and extends further and deeper underground. A large pile of mine tailings is present adjacent to the westerly end of the trench.

A rectangular ground depression which measures twelve feet by ten feet is located between the vertical water-filled shaft and Arden Valley Road. This feature is probably the remains of a mine-related structure. Several shallow exploratory pits are present in the nearby area, and the trace of an old road extends northerly from the mine openings.

Documentary information regarding the operation of the Harris Mine is extremely sparse. A map on the inside cover of Ransom's *Vanishing Ironworks of the Ramapos* shows the location of the mine around 1865. It was most likely opened and operated by the Parrott brothers to supply ore to their furnaces at present-day Arden, New York.

Figure 39: Drawing of powder storage magazine
at Cranberry Mine, 1994.

Cranberry Mine

*I*n the late 19th and early 20th centuries, extensive iron mining and exploration activity took place along the southeast side of Cranberry Hill in present-day Woodbury Township, New York. The scene of this mining activity is located north of Seven Lakes Drive near Silvermine Lake in Harriman State Park.

To find the Cranberry Mine complex (figure 40), hikers should park at the Silvermine Picnic Area and walk easterly along the north side of Seven Lakes Drive. After about half a mile, you will pass a stone comfort station on the right side of the road. Continue along the road for approximately another 500 feet to where a stream crosses under the road in a culvert. (At this point, on the right side of Seven Lakes Drive, there is a woods road which is blocked off by a cable barrier.) Turn left and follow the stream uphill for about 0.3 mile until you encounter an old woods road which runs in a general east-west direction. Turn left (west) and follow the woods road to the mine.

The principal feature of this complex is a horizontal shaft that extends into the hillside for about 200 feet. This mine opening or adit is twenty-two feet wide and about twelve feet high, while the interior shaft is twelve feet wide. A cut stone wall,

---

A nearly intact powder magazine is located near the entrance to the mine

---

bonded with cement and containing an iron plate door, was built across the entrance to the mine around 1920. The mine was used to store dynamite by park officials until the 1930s. The iron door at the mine entrance has been torn open.

The horizontal shaft extends into the hillside as a level passage for about 100 feet. Here, there is a branch shaft which goes off to the right for about 30 feet. Beyond this point, the main horizontal shaft begins to slant upwards, and it continues for about another 100 feet. A section of narrow-gauge iron rails is extant inside the mine shaft, and a piece is visible outside the entrance as well.

On the hillside above and to the west of the mine entrance is a vertical air shaft opening, about seven feet by seven feet in size, and at present about 20 feet deep. Moving further up the hillside to the west, hikers will encounter an open exploratory pit which measures twenty-two feet in length and fourteen feet in width, and which has been partially filled with stone. A tailings pile is nearby, and a road leading up to this exploration is visible.

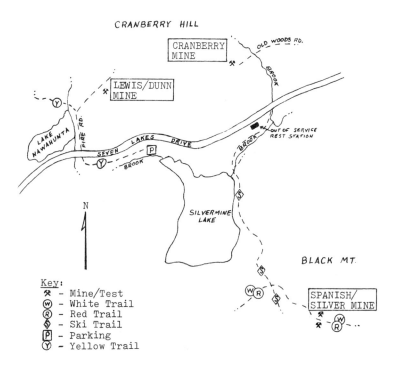

Figure 40: Map showing locations of Cranberry, Lewis and Spanish Mines.

Another exploratory test pit, seven feet by seven feet in size, is located about 450 feet to the west of the open exploratory pit.

The remains of several structures can be found in the vicinity of the mine entrance. The most significant of these is a nearly intact powder storage magazine which is located about 350 feet north of the mine shaft entrance. This former magazine is a banked earth-covered structure with interior dry-laid stone walls, a stone front with an iron door, and a domed corrugated metal roof (figure 39). The interior chamber measures fourteen feet in length and five feet in width. This powder magazine was built and used for powder storage during the period of mining activity and later was adapted for dynamite storage by the park.

The foundation of a large structure, forty-eight feet by fourteen feet, can also be seen about 150 feet north of the mine shaft entrance. This may be the site of a "corrugated steel building" which reportedly stood in this area in 1924.

A large tailings pile near the entrance to the Cranberry Mine suggests that a considerable amount of ore was removed from the mine. However, little is known about the ownership and operation of this mine. A 1902 map of this area shows a structure, a road, the nearby stream, and 3,000 acres of land belonging to R.M. Cunningham.

Lewis (Dunn) Mine

Since 1982, this mine (figure 40) has been inappropriately referred to on Trail Conference maps as the "Dunn Mine." It received this name by virtue of its accidental "discovery" by a hiker named Dunn. The mine is situated on property which once belonged to the Lewis family who resided here, farming this land in the late 19th and early 20th centuries. The Lewis family cemetery is on the south side of Seven Lakes Drive opposite the southern end of the Nawahunta Fire Road.

The Lewis Mine is located in Harriman State Park, just to the northeast of

Lake Nawahunta. To reach this mine, park at the Silvermine Picnic Area on Seven Lakes Drive. From the western end of the parking area, proceed west (parallel to Seven Lakes Drive) on the yellow-blazed Menomine Trail, which goes through a picnic area and then a pine

---

The Lewis Mine includes a trench which extends into the rock hillside

---

grove. After about a third of a mile, continue on the Menomine Trail as it turns right, crosses Seven Lakes Drive, and proceeds north along the Nawahunta Fire Road. In another 825 feet, where the yellow trail turns left and leaves the road, continue straight ahead on the road. The mine is on the right side of the road, about 675 feet north of the point where the trail leaves the road (it is about 0.3 mile north of Seven Lakes Drive). The main opening is located about seventy-five feet east of the road.

The principal feature of the Lewis workings is an open cut or trench that is twenty-eight feet long and eight feet wide. The mine extends into the rock hillside where there is a small water-filled chamber or adit. Scattered mine rock or tailings are present near the entrance to the open cut and extending to the fire road. A second open trench or mine cut may be found to the south of the main shaft along the sloping hillside and nearer the lake. This small cut is thirty feet long, varies in width and depth, and has a rock or tailing dump nearby.

The remains of a small structure are visible on the west side of the fire road overlooking the eastern end of Lake Nawahunta, about forty feet south of where the Menomine Trail leaves the fire road. It is a banked structure with an interior stone-lined chamber that measures eleven feet by ten feet with an entry way that is four feet wide on its westerly (lake) side. The walls of the structure are thick mounds of earth. This site has been described elsewhere as a cellar hole of the Lewis farmhouse. However, its size and construction features suggest that it is more likely the remains of a storage building — many similar ones have been found at other mine sites in the region.

As with the nearby Cranberry Mine, no information has come to light regarding the ownership and operation of this mine. An 1875 map of this area showing two structures indicates that the property was owned by J.H. Lewis. A subsequent 1909 map also shows the J.H. Lewis holdings, which consisted of 220.5 acres, two structures, and a road. The surface indications at the Lewis Mine suggest that very little ore was removed from this site.

Spanish Mine

*B*lack Mountain, towering more than 1,200 feet above sea level, was the scene of mining activity at some time in the remote past. Two vertical pits, evidence of attempts to extract ore, are present on the summit of this mountain which is situated to the southeast of present-day Silvermine Lake in Harriman State Park.

To reach the Spanish Mine (figure 40), hikers should park at the Silvermine Picnic Area and walk easterly along Seven Lakes Drive for about 0.4 mile until a concrete-and-stone bridge over a stream is visible 300 feet to the right of the road. (This point is about 500 feet *west* of the stone comfort station farther down the road.) Turn right and bush-whack down to the bridge, cross the bridge, and continue southward along a well-constructed woods road, known as the Silvermine Ski Road, passing along the east side of Silvermine Lake. In 0.9 mile from the bridge, you will reach a junction with the joint Appalachian/Ramapo-Dunderberg Trail (marked with white and red-dot-on-white blazes). Turn left (east), and follow this trail — steeply at first, and then more gradually — for about half a mile up to the summit of Black Mountain, passing a beautiful viewpoint over the lake.

The first mine opening is located near the summit, just north of the viewpoint at the highest point reached by the trail. This opening, which is about 100 feet north of the trail, is a vertical shaft, eight feet square and partially filled in. A small tailings pile is adjacent to the hole. The second opening is located about 250 feet farther east along the trail. This opening, another vertical shaft, is 20 feet north of the trail, and also measures eight feet by eight feet. It is about 10 feet deep, filled with water, and should be approached with extreme caution. A large tailings pile is adjacent to the hole.

A surprise awaits the intrepid hiker on the south side of Black Mountain. A

Legend claims the Spanish Mine as the burial place of Captain Kidd's treasure

---

horizontal passage or adit is located in the cliff face below the top of the mountain south-southwest of the viewpoint. This shaft is ten feet wide, nine feet high and penetrates some fifteen feet into the mountain. To find this opening, return to the Appalachian/Ramapo-Dunderberg Trail at the mountaintop viewpoint and retrace your route by hiking westerly. From the mountaintop, the trail soon descends steeply for about twenty vertical feet. At the bottom of this steep descent, turn left, leaving the trail, and continue in an easterly direction around the face of the cliff. The mine shaft is located about 100 vertical feet below the summit, so you will have to descend a little further as you proceed along the mountainside. Be careful, as the footing can be quite treacherous in this area! The opening is blasted into the rock of the mountain above the talus slope.

Facts regarding the ownership and operation of this mine, also known as the Spanish Silver Mine or the Silver Mine, are lacking, but mystery and legend abound. The 1984 edition of the *New York Walk Book* states that the Spanish Mine was the reported burial place of Captain Kidd's treasure. Another legend, attributed to R.H. Torrey, a founder of the New York-New Jersey Trail Conference, states that the mine was dug by Spanish miners in the 18th century.

According to the Torrey tale, in 1735 a ship with a Spanish crew sailed up the Hudson River and landed at what is now Jones Point. They made several trips to a mine on Black Mountain and carried out heavy sacks, once boasting to riverside tavern patrons that they were carrying silver. On their final journey to the mine, one of the Spanish crew members disappeared, while the others returned to their ship, never to be seen in the area again. Later, the body of the lost Spanish miner was found by local people in a cabin on the mountain.

This tale is one of several describing treasure hidden or found in the Highlands. Is there a kernel of truth in these stories? Ships sailed the Hudson River, pirates *were* real, and the rugged Highlands provided deep cover and secret places where legends grow.

Trace amounts of silver and gold are sometimes found in association with magnetite iron ore in the Highlands region. Hikers and rock collectors occasionally find rock specimens that appear to have a silvery metallic look. These samples usually turn out to be graphite (see, for example, the Edison Mine at Doodletown). Did the early prospectors find a small pocket of silver at the Spanish Mine site, or were they fooled by the silvery appearance of graphite?

Hasenclever Mine

*I*n the mid-19th century, an investment prospectus referred to the Hasenclever Mine as "one of the most valuable iron mines in America." Today, the mine complex consists of shafts, pits, foundations, tailing piles and other features within a beautiful forest setting. The Hasenclever Mine is located southeast of Lake Tiorati in Harriman State Park. The mine is situated on the Red Cross Trail about one-half mile south of Tiorati Brook Road. The trail follows the old wagon road, known as the Hasenclever Road, to the site (figure 41). Here, the main Hasenclever Road goes off to the left, while the Red Cross Trail follows a fire road to the right.

There are two large mine openings at the site. The principal one, on the east side of the road, is a water-filled hole that is seventy-five feet long and twenty-five feet wide and reported to be 100 feet deep. The second is located about 250 feet further along the Red Cross Trail, on the north side of the trail, and is a T-shaped open cut or trench. This mine cut is eighty-three feet long and thirty feet wide, parallel to the old road (now the Red Cross Trail), and is filled with 20th century park-era trash, such as coal, ash, ceramic and glass fragments, tin cans, bone scraps, metal containers of various sizes and other materials. An open trench 100 feet long and fifteen feet wide extends in a northerly direction from the trash-filled pit. Another trash-filled pit, measuring about twenty-three feet in length, seventeen feet in width and presently six feet deep, is located twenty feet to the east of the T-shaped cut described above.

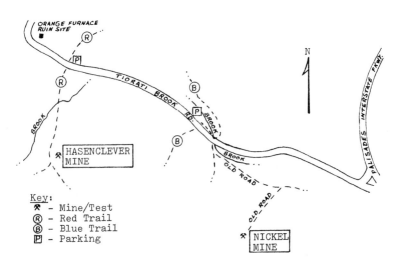

Figure 41: Map showing locations of Hasenclever and Nickel Mines.

Several small exploratory pits can be seen near the junction of the Red Cross Trail and a fire road adjacent to the west side of the water-filled hole. These pits are shallow and dry; one is

The Hasenclever Mine: "One of the most valuable iron mines in America."

located on the west side of the trail with an adjacent tailings pile, and two are on the east side of the trail. A deep cut or shaft twenty-one feet by eleven feet is located on the westerly side of the fire road, directly opposite the south end of the water-filled mine hole.

One of the most significant features at the Hasenclever Mine site is a long and deep trench which begins about ninety-two feet north of the main water-filled shaft and extends in a westerly direction. This dry open cut is 450 feet long, twenty feet wide and about eight feet deep. Spoil piles of earth are present on both sides of the trench. The floor of the trench reaches ground level at its westerly end, and becomes a raised roadbed which turns northerly and extends some 237 feet, ending abruptly in a wetland area. This open trench-roadbed was planned in 1854 as a narrow-gauge railroad line which would connect the mine with other operations on the Hudson River.

A road built of mine rock connects the east end of the planned narrow-gauge railroad line with the north end of the T-shaped mine cut previously described. This roadbed extends from north to south for about 200 feet, and can be traced all the way to the main woods road. A dry-laid stone foundation, twenty-five feet by twenty-one feet, is situated along the east side of this road. Numerous large piles of iron ore and rock have been dumped along the west side of the main mine road just north of the principal, now water-filled, shaft. Mine rock is also present on the east side of the road immediately to the north of the mine. One large stone block near the mine has a drilled hole which contains the broken protruding remains of an iron drill.

The foundation of a large structure is located about 300 feet to the north of the mine on the west side of the old road. This structure is fifty-three feet long by twenty-five feet wide and has a partial stone-lined cellar in its center. An eighteen-foot-by-fourteen-foot stone foundation abuts the west side of the structure. Brick fragments are present on the surface of the ground. The function of this former building is unknown. The remains of a small storage building are located

> **By 1855, twenty to thirty men were employed at the Hasenclever Mine**

eight feet east of the northeast corner of the structure just described. This is a banked structure with a dry-stone interior chamber that is nine feet by six feet with an entrance that faces east, towards the road. This structure may have been a powder storage magazine.

The Hasenclever iron ore deposit was discovered and initially developed in 1765 by Peter Hasenclever, who purchased 1,000 acres of land, including the site, for the purpose of establishing an ironworks on the nearby Cedar Ponds (now Tiorati) Brook. Peter Hasenclever was an iron entrepreneur who headed a group of British investors known as the London Company. This company established and operated mines, furnaces, and forges at Ringwood, Long Pond and Charlotteburg, New Jersey, and at Cortlandt, New York, and "intended" to build a works at Cedar Ponds (now Lake Tiorati in Harriman State Park). Hasenclever dammed Cedar Ponds, forming a large reservoir for providing power, built log houses and a road, and started to build a blast furnace which was never completed because of financial difficulties.

During the Revolutionary War, the Hasenclever iron mine property was leased and worked by Samuel Brewster. In 1799, the 1,000-acre mine tract, plus an adjoining 332-acre tract which included Cedar Ponds (now Lake Tiorati) and the outlet brook, were purchased by Jonas Brewster. A blast furnace was erected on Cedar Ponds

(Tiorati) Brook around 1800 by Samuel and Jonas Brewster. The ruins of this operation can be seen today on the southwestern bank of the brook just above the Red Cross Trail crossing.

Following the deaths of Jonas and Samuel Brewster, and subsequent to 1821, the mining lot property changed hands several times. In 1854, a lease to the property was acquired by the Haverstraw Iron and Mining Company, which began to mine the ore and build a railroad to its furnaces on the Hudson River. By 1855, twenty to thirty men were employed at the mine, and five to eight thousand tons of ore had been removed and awaited shipment. However, by 1856 the Haverstraw Iron and Mining Company's mine venture failed.

Following the collapse of the Haverstraw Iron and Mining Company, the Hasenclever Mine was acquired and worked by four subsequent owners. It was last worked around 1891 by A. Lawrence Edmonds, who was associated with Thomas Edison in developing iron mining properties.

Nickel Mine

Nickel-iron, often found in meteors, is an excellent raw material for use in the iron and steel industries, but its use is limited because of its rare occurrence in terrestrial rock. This ore normally occurs in gray or black masses, sheets, or tiny grains present in other minerals. It is formed in rock by the reduction of iron oxides contained in basalts that have come into contact with carbonate rocks. Nickel-iron is hard and strongly magnetic.

The Nickel Mine (figure 41) is located on Grape Swamp Mountain in Harriman State Park. To reach the site, hikers should leave their cars at the parking area on Tiorati Brook Road at the Beech Trail crossing and proceed east for about 750 feet on the Beech Trail, parallel to the road. Where the trail crosses the brook on the road bridge, go to the south side of the road and follow an old road which begins to run along the south side of the brook. This road, known as the Grape Swamp

Mountain Trail, is badly overgrown in several places. Ignore the first branch road that goes off to the right in a few hundred feet, and continue east along the road, which soon leaves the brook. After about half a mile, at a junction marked by cairns, another branch of the road turns sharply to the right and proceeds up the steep hillside. Turn right here and continue up this road for about another half a mile until you reach the mine site. Stone cairns have been placed at several locations along this hillside trail to aid hikers in finding the way. However, this mine site is best visited in late fall and in winter, when the ground surface visibility is at its best.

The Nickel Mine consists primarily of four open trenches or pits. The first of these is encountered at the top of the trail and is eighty feet long, five to seven feet wide, and about six feet deep. The second open pit is located fifty feet southwest of the first. It is a T-shaped open trench; its stem extends from north to south and is sixty feet long and six to eight feet wide. At its south end, the top of the "T," the trench extends from east to west and is eighty-seven feet long, twenty-seven feet wide, and twenty feet deep.

A small exploratory pit is located on the hillside about 150 feet to the east of the

---

The Nickel Mine is named for nickel-iron, a very hard and strongly magnetic ore

---

large open trench cuts. This pit is seventeen feet in length, eleven feet in width, and four feet in depth. A small earth and rock pile is adjacent to the north side of this dry, shallow exploration.

A large mine dump is present in the area between the two open trenches. Mine tailings are also present on the hilltop on the south side of the T-shaped open pit.

Two additional mine openings are located to the west of those just described. To find these openings, start at the western end of the T-shaped trench. Take a compass bearing west and hike along the top of the ridge for about 550 feet to the third large open pit. This pit is rectangular with slightly rounded ends, and it extends from east to west for forty feet. It is fifteen feet wide and eight feet in depth to its water-filled bottom. Rock and ore tailings extend along the south side of this open pit, with an extensive L-shaped mine dump to the north.

The fourth mine opening is an open pit or trench located fifty feet west of the one described above. This trench, open on its western end, is thirty-five feet long, nine feet wide and ten feet deep. A flat, level area on the south side of the trench consists of crushed mine rock and probably served as a working surface for mining equipment. Mine rock and tailings are present on the north side of the pit and about fifteen feet north-northwest of the opening.

Cole's *History of Rockland County* (1884) indicates that this mine was opened in 1871 and that a "considerable" quantity of nickel ore had been removed from the site. However, the physical evidence at the site does not support the claim of "considerable" mining and extraction of ore. The mine

property is located in the Great Mountain Lot No. 2 of the Cheesecocks Patent. It was owned by Brewster J. Allison who referred to it as the Bulson Lot. Cole's history states that a mining lease was given to John Sneviley of New York City. In 1875, the mining rights were purchased by the Rockland Nickel Company of New York City, whose president was Emory Rider. By 1884, the mine was no longer in operation.

Barnes Mine

*T*he Barnes Mine (figure 42) is located on the southern slope of Pole Brook Mountain and is on the north side of Lake Welch Drive in Harriman State Park. It is situated about 0.2 mile to the east of the intersection of St. John's Road and Lake Welch Drive; a large and formidable mine dump is clearly visible from the road, and a stone wall leads from the mine dump down the hillside to the road. An old road begins on the northwest side of Lake Welch Drive a short distance to the east of the mine. If one follows this road up the hillside for about 150 feet, an old abandoned mine road is visible to the left. This road leads up the hillside to the mine site.

The main feature of this mine is a large cruciform-shaped open pit from which rock and ore have been extracted. This north-to-south cut measures eighty-three feet in length and varies in width from ten to thirteen feet. At the extreme north end of this cut, the excavation is somewhat wider and deeper. Here the mine pit undercuts the rock ledge and contains water. The east-to-west crossing mine cut is 113 feet in total length, and thirteen to seventeen feet wide. A large pile of tailings is situated adjacent to the southeast side of the mine entrance. There is a large flat area — the mine dump visible from Lake Welch Drive — located

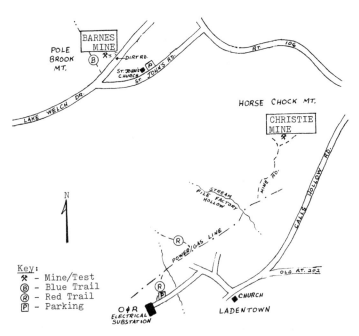

Figure 42: Map showing locations of Barnes and Christie Mines.

directly south of the entrance to the mine.

A shallow exploratory pit, ten feet by eight feet in size, is located seventy feet to the north of the mine. Another shallow test pit, twelve feet by eight feet, is located thirty-five feet west of the north end of the mine. The remains of a small structure, possibly a powder storage area, can be seen at a point 250 feet northeast of the mine. It appears to have had a stone-lined interior chamber that measured eight feet by six feet, thick earthen walls and an entrance on its easterly side.

According to trail historian Myles, the mine lot property consisting of seventeen acres was purchased in 1846 by Isaac Barnes. In 1864, the property was owned by John Charleston, who leased the mine to the Rockland Nickel Company in 1871. Historian Bedell (1941) states that the Barnes Mine ceased operating about 1880. This mine does not appear to have been extensively worked.

The Barnes Mine is inextricably linked to the Charleston family, which once lived in the Sandyfields-Johnsontown area near what is now Lake Welch and St. John's-in-the-Wilderness Church. Charleston family oral history states that Jerome Charleston, as a young man, worked in the mine in the late 19th century. The mine reportedly provided a source of income for Jerome and his brother Milton. They sold the iron ore, described as deep red in color, to the brick yards in Haverstraw, New York, to be ground and used as a coloring ingredient in bricks. This description of the ore suggests that it was red hematite.

Christie Mine

The Christie Mine (figure 42) is situated on the southeastern slope of Horse Chock Mountain in the Town of Haverstraw, Rockland County, New York. The site is near the eastern border of Harriman State Park and just west of Calls Hollow Road. A hike to the Christie Mine will provide the curious and careful observer with a new perspective of early settlement and industrial activity in this once-remote region. The existence of this mine demonstrates the extent to which people pushed themselves to mine iron ore. Upon reaching the site, imagine what it must have

---

The Christie Mine is a deep open pit, cut into the steep slope of a mountain ravine

---

been like to transport ore down the mountain for processing elsewhere. Imagine what it was like to live and work on this steep hillside.

The route to the Christie Mine begins at the southern terminus of the red-dash-on-white-blazed Tuxedo-Mt. Ivy Trail. To reach this point, take Route 202 north to the intersection of Route 306 in Ladentown, and turn left onto Old Route 202. Continue for 0.2 mile to Mountain Road and turn left, then turn left again in another 0.2 mile onto a private road. Continue for 0.2 mile until you see a sign for hikers' parking on the right side of the road. Park here and take the Tuxedo-Mt. Ivy Trail north to

its junction with an overhead power line and contiguous gas line. Here the red trail turns right and follows the overhead power line and underground gas line, which parallel each other, in a northerly direction. After 0.3 mile, the trail turns left and crosses under the power line. Immediately afterwards, it reaches the power line service road. Turn right at this point, leaving the Tuxedo-Mt. Ivy Trail, and continue north along the power line service road.

A walk of about a mile brings you to a fast-flowing mountain stream coming down a steep ravine known as File Factory Hollow. Here, immediately to the left of the power line service road, one can see the remains of an old stone dam which once impounded the stream to provide power to the mills below.

Continue heading north along the power line service road. In another 0.6 mile, you will pass an abandoned concrete, earth, and stone-banked structure to the left. This building was probably a storage facility during the construction of the power and/or gas lines. About 0.2 mile beyond the abandoned building, you will come to a deep ravine between two mountain ridges (Horse Chock Mountain on the north and Iron Mountain on the south). Turn left, and follow an old mine road up the left side of the steep ravine to the principal Christie Mine opening.

The Christie Mine is a deep open pit, cut into the side of the mountain within the ravine, measuring forty feet in length, sixteen feet in width and six feet to fifteen

---

The mine's remoteness shows the extreme difficulties miners were willing to endure

---

feet in depth. A rock dump, the overburden from this excavation, is present along the southwesterly side of the pit. A network of old roads surround the mine opening. At the southeast or open end of the mine pit, there is a stone bridge, and the mine road crosses the ravine and continues up the hillside to the north. A branch road goes off in a northwesterly-

westerly direction from the stone bridge, and continues along the left side of the ravine, rising steeply up the hillside past the mine. Directly below, or southeast of the bridge, is a channel with laid-up stone walls on each side. This channel is seven feet wide and thirty-two feet long. Its function is unclear. At the end of the channel and extending downslope for about forty-three feet is a large mine dump. The physical layout suggests that the channel might have been the working entrance to the mine and the means by which ore and rock debris were removed from the workings. If this was the case, then the stone bridge was a later construction at the site. This puzzle remains to be solved.

A second mine opening, a shallow trench, is located about 100 feet south of, and somewhat lower on the hillside from, the large open pit described above. This trench is thirty-five feet long, seven feet wide and three feet deep. A small section of laid-up stonework is present along one side of the trench at its lower end. The ruins of a

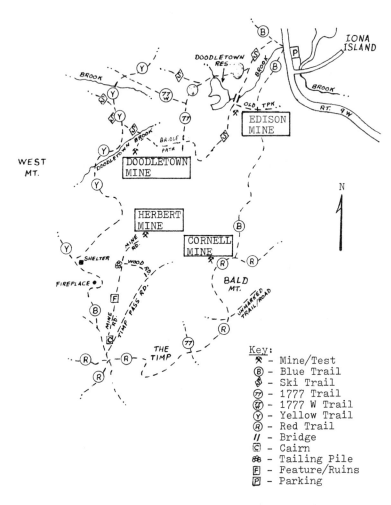

Figure 43: Map showing locations of Doodletown, Cornell, Herbert and Edison Mines.

structure are also present here, consisting of wooden boards, asphalt roofing, sheet metal fragments and fragments of bottle glass.

The documentary record regarding the Christie Mine is meager. An 1876 "Map of Haverstraw Township" by F.A. Davis shows an "Iron Mine" on Horse Chock Mountain owned by the "Christie Mining Co."

Doodletown Mine

*T*he abandoned hamlet of Doodletown lies in a beautiful valley surrounded by Bear Mountain on the north, Bald Mountain and Dunderberg Mountain on the south and southeast, and West Mountain on the west. Since the 18th century, this valley has been the scene of settlement, farming, Revolutionary War activity and mining. The Doodletown Mine (figure 43) is located on the northern slope of West Mountain in Bear Mountain State Park, Rockland County, New York, about 0.2 mile east of the crossing of Doodletown Brook by the yellow-blazed Suffern-Bear Mountain Trail.

To reach the Doodletown Mine, hikers should park in the small parking area on the east side of Route 9W just north of the entrance to Iona Island. Cross the highway bridge over the Doodletown Brook, and follow the blue-blazed Cornell Mine Trail uphill as it heads north on the old Doodletown Road (now abandoned and blocked off by large boulders). After about 750 feet, just after the road bends sharply to the left, the blue-blazed trail leaves to the right. Continue ahead (southwest) on the old road, paralleling Doodletown Brook, which is to the left or southeast. In about another 0.3 mile, you will notice a large sign with the number "9." Here, the 1777E Trail joins from the right. Continue ahead, following the 1777E Trail. After about half a mile, the 1777W Trail joins from the right, and the joint trail becomes known as the 1777 Trail. Proceed ahead for another 0.3 mile until a woods road crosses at a numbered sign. Here you turn right onto the woods road, known as the Doodletown Bridle Path, and continue for about 0.3 mile. About 200 feet before the Bridle Path crosses a stream (Doodletown Brook), an old road is vaguely visible to the left. This old road, marked in places with cairns, leads for a quarter of a mile to the mine, which may be identified by a large pile of tailings to the left. Climb the tailings pile to reach the mine.

The mine consists of an open trench cut into the rock hillside following a north-to-south course. The cut is 100 feet long and expands to a width of fifteen feet at its south end. The south end of the cut is twenty-six feet deep; at the bottom is a water-filled shaft of unknown depth. Drill holes are in evidence in the rock walls of the mine. A short distance to the east is a small exploratory pit. A large flat pile of tailings is located at the entrance to the mine. A second mine dump, also flattened, is situated below and to the north of the mine entrance.

A dry-stone foundation is present along the road just below the mine. This cellar hole measures fourteen feet by seven feet and has an entry way on its westerly side.

The ownership and period of operation of the Doodletown Mine are not known. However, it is likely that the mine was active in the 19th century. The size and depth of the mine cut and the two large dumps suggest that a sizeable amount of ore was removed from the mine.

Cornell Mine

The Cornell Mine (figure 43) consists of several open pits, trenches, and shafts located along the northern slope and top of Bald Mountain in Bear Mountain State Park, Rockland County, New York. An exploratory hike to these sites is extremely rewarding as several vistas of the Hudson Valley are encountered along the way, with the view from the top of Bald Mountain being particularly magnificent.

To reach the Cornell Mine, take the blue-blazed Cornell Mine Trail south from the hikers' parking area located on the east side of Route 9W just north of the entrance to Iona Island. For the first mile, the trail alternates between moderate grades and relatively flat stretches. Then the trail steeply ascends Bald Mountain, climbing about 600 vertical feet in 0.4 mile. Near the top of the mountain, the Cornell Mine Trail ends at an intersection with the red-dot-on-white-blazed Ramapo-Dunderberg Trail.

The first mine opening is encountered along the Cornell Mine Trail at approximately the 620-foot elevation, just before the trail bears left. Here, immediately to the right of the trail, is an open trench thirty-six feet long by eight feet wide, with a few tailings nearby. A short distance further along the trail (*i.e.*, up the mountain), at about the 820-foot elevation, there is a large open pit cut into the side of the hill. The mine opening, which is also on the right side of the trail, is keyhole-shaped and measures forty-eight feet in length, thirteen feet in width and twelve feet in depth. Large tailing piles are located adjacent to the pit.

At the intersection of the Cornell Mine and Ramapo-Dunderberg Trails there is an exploratory pit that is ten feet in diameter. Here one should turn right and proceed uphill along the Ramapo-Dunderberg Trail. After a short distance, the trail bears left. At this point, the hiker should leave the trail and continue straight ahead for about 150 feet. Here, cut into the hillside to the left, is an impressive horizontal shaft. This adit or shaft opening is five feet by five feet and extends into the hillside about fifty feet; it should not be entered, as it contains water and is dangerous. There is an open cut twenty

---

A hike to this site is extremely rewarding, offering sweeping vistas of the Hudson Valley

---

feet in length leading to the horizontal shaft, and a large tailings pile is present nearby. On the hillside, just above the horizontal shaft, is a circular open pit twenty feet in diameter. This circular pit has an entry way ten feet in length on its downslope side with an adjacent tailings pile.

After exploring these features, the hiker should return to the trail and continue up to the top of Bald Mountain. At the top of the mountain, there is a water-filled vertical mine shaft. This shaft is thirteen feet in diameter, and its depth from the ground surface to the water level is twelve feet. A large tailings pile is located nearby. A small, shallow test pit is located just south of the shaft to the left of the Ramapo-Dunderberg Trail.

The Cornell Mine workings are situated within a tract of land granted by King George III to William Kempe, James Lamb, and

> **The Cornell Mine was probably dug prior to 1859, and ceased operation by 1890**

John Crum in 1769. An irregular tract of land consisting of 3,000 acres, it is referred to as the Kempe Patent on Pellatreau's 1884 Rockland County patent map. In 1874, a 175-acre parcel of the original patent including Bald Mountain was owned by Minerva Herbert. According to Myles' *Harriman Trails*,

Minerva Herbert leased her property for a period of twenty years to Alexander Phyfe of New York City. In 1885, Thomas Cornell of Kingston, New York, acquired the lease rights to mine iron ore on the property. Cornell reportedly hired an individual named Baldwin to operate his mine interests.

Myles also states that the upper two mine openings on Bald Mountain were probably dug prior to 1859, and the lower pits were dug between 1885 and 1890. The Cornell Mine ceased operating in 1890, and the property was sold to William B. Tramaine, who in turn sold it to David B. Sickels in 1893.

In 1890, inventor Thomas A. Edison acquired a 197.59-acre tract which included the northeast side of Bald Mountain up to an elevation of approximately 500 feet above sea level. Edison, who was developing an extensive iron ore separating and concentrating works at Ogdensburg, New Jersey, undoubtedly acquired this property as a potential source of ore for his new venture. There is evidence of mining activity on Edison's property (see the description of the Edison Mine, *infra*).

Although the Cornell Mine was sold in 1890 and again in 1893, Edison apparently made no attempt to acquire this mine property.

Herbert Mine

*T*he Herbert Mine (figure 43) is an extensive complex of mining features located on the southeastern slope of West Mountain in Harriman State Park. It consists of three open pits, the foundation of a dwelling, the remains of a banked storage chamber, tailing piles, and a connecting road network. The principal mine opening is at an elevation of approximately 900 feet above mean sea level, and the surrounding rock outcrop is easily distinguishable by its dull black color.

To reach the Herbert Mine, take the blue-blazed Timp-Torne Trail from Route 9W, just south of Jones Point

Road. (Cars may be parked in an open area adjacent to the intersection.) This interesting trail incorporates features of the never-completed Dunderberg Spiral Railway — including two tunnels — and affords a number of magnificent views. After about three miles, the red-dot-on-white-blazed Ramapo-Dunderberg Trail crosses, and the Timp-Torne Trail soon reaches the summit of The Timp, whose open rock ledges offer excellent views to the north and west. The trail then descends steeply from The Timp to Timp Pass Road.

Here, the Timp-Torne Trail turns left. To reach the mine, turn *right* onto the unmarked Timp Pass Road and descend for 0.4 mile until you encounter an outcrop of bedrock on the left which has been marked by a stone cairn. Turn left here, cross a wet area, and you will come to the beginning of an old mine road. Follow this old mine road in a northerly direction as it gradually ascends the hillside. The road is easily distinguishable as it was well laid-out. It is a substantial path, and portions of it are supported on the downslope side by laid-up stonework. Ore wagons could easily have travelled along this route. The road leads up to a flat, cleared mountainside terrace that contains two cultural features: the foundations of a structure and of a storage facility.

Considerable effort was expended clearing this terrace. Stone piles placed on bedrock are evidence of land clearing. Near the south-central part of the terrace is a square ground

> **The Herbert Mine is an extensive complex with three open pits and structural remains**

depression with low earth-mounded sides. This feature measures eighteen feet by eighteen feet and was probably the foundation of a small cabin or similar structure. Thirty-eight feet to the east of the small foundation, along the edge of the terrace, is the collapsed ruin of a stone chamber which was used for storage. The interior of the chamber was constructed of dry-laid stone and the walls were banked with earth. This storage chamber measures twelve feet by five feet and its opening faces to the east. This terrace and its former structures were once a work-staging area for the mine.

Continue your hike to the mine by heading north along the terrace and following the mine road again along the hillside. At a distance of approximately 850 feet north of the foundation on the terrace, you will come to a large pile of mine tailings on the uphill side of the road. This material was clearly brought down the mountainside from the mine openings above. At this tailings pile, the road divides — one branch heads left or up the mountain, while the other turns right and descends. Take the road leading up the steep hillside to the main mine excavation.

The Herbert Mine consists of two exploratory pits dug into the rock hillside. The main opening is thirty feet long, thirty feet wide and about seven feet high along the rear rock face. There is a smaller open pit located immediately to the west and slightly uphill that measures twenty-two feet by seventeen feet and twelve feet in height along its rear wall. A large tailings pile is situated immediately

---

It appears that a substantial effort was made to find iron ore in this location

---

in front of these exploratory pits. It appears that a substantial effort was made to find iron ore in this location.

Continue up the steep hillside heading west along a barely visible road until you come to another flat terrace which contains a small wetland area and pond. Near the edge of this pond is another small exploratory pit that is ten feet by ten feet and two feet deep. A pile of black rock tailings lies nearby. (In fact, much of the rock outcrop in this area is dull black in color.) At this point, retrace your steps, heading down

the hillside to the first isolated tailings pile mentioned earlier. From this tailings pile, follow an eroded roadbed down the hillside to where it joins the Timp Pass Road. Turn left and follow the road northeast and then east until Timp Pass Road ends at Pleasant Valley Road, which is the route of the red-blazed 1777 Trail. Turn right and head south along this trail for about two-thirds of a mile to its intersection with the blue-blazed Timp-Torne Trail, then turn left and return to your car by heading east along the Timp-Torne Trail.

Historian James M. Ransom states that the Herbert Mine was opened before 1859 and was named after a family of that name who lived in nearby Doodletown. The 1859 *Map of Orange and Rockland Counties* by French, Wood and Beers shows an unidentified "Iron Mine" located about half a mile west-southwest of Doodletown. The 1876 *Map of Stony Point Township* by F.A. Davis shows the "Herbert Mines" and "Iron Mines" in the same location. The mines shown on the 1859 and 1876 maps most likely refer to the Doodletown Mine described earlier. The Herbert Mine described here is about one mile south-southwest of the junction of Doodletown Road and Pleasant Valley Road in the abandoned hamlet of Doodletown.

Edison Mine

*I*n 1890, inventor Thomas A. Edison purchased 197.59 acres of land located on the north slope of Dunderberg Mountain and at the base of Bald Mountain, near Doodletown in the Town of Stony Point, Rockland County, New York.

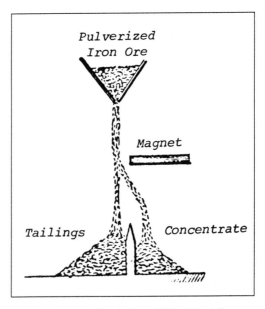

Figure 44: Illustration of "The Principle of Edison's Magnetic Concentrator."

The exploration for suitable ore deposits on this property was handled by one of Edison's subsidiary business enterprises, the New York Concentrating Works. In 1890, this company, which Edison served as president and Charles A. Batchelor as general manager, leased the abandoned Sunk Mines in Putnam County, east of the Hudson River, and placed Edison's magnetic ore separators into use at these mines.

Two years earlier, in 1888, Edison had developed a technique for producing concentrated high-quality magnetite iron ore (figure 44). His method included crushing and pulverizing large quantities of ore, then using electromagnets to separate the iron particles from waste material and concentrating the iron into briquettes which could be shipped to blast furnaces for the production of steel. Through this method, Edison hoped to revive the moribund iron mine industry in the New York-New Jersey region.

In order to facilitate his new venture, Edison ex-plored potential iron mine sites throughout the northeast. He sent out teams of prospectors-surveyors to search for magnetite iron ore deposits. By 1893, Edison

Thomas Edison hoped to revive Highlands iron mining by using his ore concentrator

had purchased or leased 145 mining tracts, including the property at Doodletown. Edison apparently prospected for ore within his Doodletown property. A mine shaft and other associated features were found within his lands in 1993 by this author and several colleagues.

The Edison Mine (figure 43) is located southeast of the Doodletown Reservoir; it is situated south of the abandoned Old Turnpike between the Cornell Mine Trail on the east and the Doodletown Bridle Path (now a ski trail) on the west. (On the 1995 edition of Trail Conference Map #4, this mine is inappropriately designated as the Lost Tom Mine.) To reach this mine, hikers should park in the small parking area on the east side of Route 9W just north of the entrance to Iona Island. Cross the highway bridge over the Doodletown Brook, and follow the blue-blazed Cornell Mine Trail uphill as

---

The Edison Mine consists of a single downward sloping mine shaft

---

it heads north on the old Doodletown Road (now abandoned and blocked off by large boulders). After about 750 feet, just after the road bends sharply to the left, the blue-blazed trail leaves to the right. Continue ahead (southwest) on the old road, paralleling Doodletown Brook, which is to the left or southeast. In about another 0.3 mile, you will notice a large sign with the number "9." Here, the Doodletown Bridle Path comes in from the right and, after about 65 feet, goes down to the left (there is a second sign with the number "9" at this point). Turn left onto the Bridle

Path (shown on the Conference map as a ski trail) here, and descend to Doodletown Brook, which is crossed on a stone bridge. In another 750 feet, with the dam of the Doodletown Reservoir immediately to the right, the Bridle Path reaches a junction with the abandoned Old Turnpike (a dirt road), which goes off to the left. Continue southwest along the Bridle Path for another 750 feet, and scan the hillside to your left, looking for the telltale sign of the mine — a pile of mine tailings located about 100 feet up the hillside to the east of the Bridle Path.

The Edison Mine consists of a downward-sloping shaft that extends thirty-six feet in a northeasterly direction. The shaft opening at the surface measures eighteen feet by eleven feet and the maximum vertical depth is ten feet. Piles of mine rock are present on the north and west sides of the shaft. Several drill holes are visible on the rock walls inside the mine shaft. A sample of what was believed to be ore was removed from the mine shaft in 1993 by this author for analysis; later examination determined that it was graphite schist and not iron.

There is a small pile of ore located about thirty feet southeast of the mine opening. Also, there is a flat platform, constructed of rock and earth with laid-up stonework on its west side, that is located about eighty feet south of the mine shaft. This platform probably served as a base for mining equipment on this sloping hillside. The physical evidence at the site indicates that this mine was an exploratory venture and was not operated commercially.

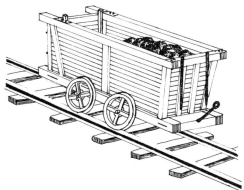

Figure 45: Drawing of ore car on narrow-gauge track.

Figure 46: Silhouette of a miner and mine picks.
(Adapted from Harper's New Monthly Magazine, 1860.)
The pick in the miner's hand depicts an actual specimen found at the
ruins of a cottage located near the Winston and Whritenour Mines.
The pick at the right was found at the Long Pond Ironworks. It is
stamped with the letters "TIC," the mark of the Trenton Iron Company.

The Archaeology of Mining in the Highlands

*T*he documentary and field survey data presented in this book have enabled us to develop an historical picture or model of iron mining in the northern Highlands region. Our archaeological observations included documenting the most visible features in the mining sites discussed here, such as adits, shafts, pits, trenches, tailing piles, roads and the remains of buildings. We examined the archaeological record and noted such details as where these features are found, what their physical characteristics are, and how they are distributed over the landscape. Some inferences have been drawn about the extent of mining activity at these sites and the length of time during which they were operated. From these field observations and the documentary record we have developed a model of mining site structure in the Highlands, which is presented here.

Mining activity in the northern Highlands region was relatively small scale and closely tied to the production capacity of nearby furnaces, forges and bloomeries. The mine sites are "clusters" of excavations or workings, tailing piles or dumps, and small banked structures, probably powder storage magazines. For the most part, settlements and house sites are lacking. The exceptions are the Hogencamp and Pine Swamp Mines in Harriman State Park, which contain some elements of mining camps or residential settlement. Large mining villages are also found elsewhere in the region such as at Ringwood, New Jersey, and Sterling, New York (presently private lands and not discussed in this book).

From these data we infer that mining activity at a typical site was limited to prospecting, blasting, excavation of the ore, and shipping ore to processing sites elsewhere. The data suggests that the miners, teamsters and other workers did not live on site, or that the remains of their dwellings were impermanent, temporary and are no longer visible on the landscape. In one case, at the Whritenour Mine in the Monksville area of New Jersey, an oral history account indicates that the mine workers were local people who resided or boarded on nearby farms. The implication is that mining activity, at least at this site, was not a full-time occupation. Residential activity seems to have occurred elsewhere.

Activity areas and artifacts of camps and settlements are not present at the mine sites described herein. Trash dumps, privies or other indications of human activity associated with mining settlements have not been found. The absence of household trash is particularly puzzling and raises several questions: Where did the miners prepare and consume their meals? Where did they sleep? Were areas set aside as latrines or privies? Did the miners dispose of their trash within the mines? Were tools and machinery as well as refuse left behind in the underground caverns and pits? Any surviving artifacts or cultural features in the underground workings themselves may represent valuable archaeological resources. However, for obvious reasons of safety, attempts to locate underground mine features should *not* be undertaken. Regrettably, we know little about the lifeways of miners: the nature of their households, consumption patterns, trade networks and other aspects of their daily lives.

Inferences regarding the technology employed at the various sites are limited by the data at hand. Although there is ample evidence of adits, shafts, pits, tailings and waste dumps, other technological features are generally lacking. Concrete engine pads with iron tie rods and iron pipes are visible at the Hogencamp, Greenwood and Surebridge Mines in Harriman State Park, which indicates that steam power was employed for drilling, dewatering, and probably hoisting. Deep drill holes, present at many sites, indicate mechanical drilling run by compressed air. Ruins of solidly-buttressed, banked powder magazines reveal the care with which the blasting powder was handled. Finally, sections of narrow-gauge iron rails on which ore carts travelled were found at the Hogencamp and Cranberry Mines in Harriman State Park, New York, and at the Patterson Mine in New Jersey, giving evidence of transport.

Mining machinery is absent at the mine sites in the Highlands. It appears that all usable equipment and supplies were removed and salvaged when mining operations ceased. Buildings, if present, were probably moved or torn down. Scavenging by local residents following the abandonment of the mines — as well as the activities of modern-day relic collectors — also accounts for the lack of evidence of mining technology.

The typical mining cycle in the Highlands region was one of prospecting, excavation of iron ore, cessation of operations, reopening of the mines, and final abandonment. The duration of this cycle and the period of time between each phase was dictated by the quality of the ore found, the difficulty and cost of extracting the ore, the cost of transportation, the market demand for this raw material, and economic conditions in the industry in general (*i.e.*, cost, profitability).

This discontinuous cycle resulted in the physical alteration or destruction of earlier mining components at each site. Previously-existing structural features were often reworked or partially destroyed, although they sometimes survived intact. Reopening the mines resulted in the development of new structures and features. Abandonment of the site presents a final episode of mining activity which is a blending of elements of previous phases. This final picture is observed by historians, archaeologists and hikers alike.

Epilogue

*T*his book is not intended to be a comprehensive history of iron mining in the northern Highlands region. Its purpose is simply to stimulate interest in, and enjoyment of, these long-abandoned ruins of our industrial past, and to be a trail guide to mine ruins — informative and enjoyable. We have combined documentary information with field survey data to produce an image of early mining activity in areas that are now hidden and remote.

Research on iron mines is always open-ended and continual; new data produces new interpretations and conclusions. New facts often result in more mysteries and questions than they were intended to answer.

Iron Mine Trails would not have been written if not for the encouragement and support of my friends and colleagues Thomas Fitzpatrick and Nancy L. Gibbs. Tom and Nancy were enthusiastic participants in field exploration work, research and site analysis. Tom produced the excellent maps and marvelous drawings for this book, and Nancy edited the manuscript and suggested many improvements. I owe them a major debt of thanks.

Over the years, several individuals have assisted in the field reconnaissance and recording of iron mine sites. I am grateful for the tremendous assistance given to me by Ronald J. Dupont, Jr., Rick Patterson, and Kevin Olsen.

Research and technical assistance has been generously provided by Michelle Figliomeni and the Orange County Historical Society, William Trusewicz, Jack Chard, George Sellmer and Bierce Riley.

Special thanks are also due to Nancy L. Gibbs, Mead Stapler, and Ronald J. Dupont, Jr. for reviewing and commenting on the draft manuscript of this book. This book would not have been possible without the generous help of Ronald J. Dupont, Jr., who typed the manuscript.

Finally, I would like to thank Daniel D. Chazin, who edited my manuscript on behalf of the New York-New Jersey Trail Conference. Dan was no desk-bound editor; he test-hiked most of these routes. We often wrangled over his suggestions, but his efforts have added to the accuracy of the directions and the clarity of the text.

Figure 47: Dickerson Mine, circa 1860.
(Harper's New Monthly Magazine, 1860.)

Bibliography

Bayley, William S.
1910   *Iron Mines and Mining in New Jersey.* Geological
         Survey of New Jersey, Trenton, New Jersey.

Bedell, Cornelia F.
1941   *Now and Then and Long Ago in Rockland County.*
         Privately printed. New York.

Beers, F.W.
1875   *Outline Plan of Orange County, New York.* F.W. Beers
         & Co., New York.

1875   "Monroe." In *Atlas of Orange County, New York.* F.W.
         Beers & Co., New York.

1891   *Atlas of the Hudson River Valley from New York City
         to Troy, Section II, Portion of Orange & Rockland
         County.* Watson & Co., Publisher, New York.

Bergen County Historic Sites Survey
1984   *Township of Mahwah.* Volume 2. Bergen County
         Board of Chosen Freeholders, Bergen County Office of
         Cultural and Historic Affairs, Bergen County Historic
         Sites Advisory Board.

Cohen, David S.
1974   *The Ramapo Mountain People.* Rutgers University
         Press, New Brunswick, New Jersey.

Cole, David
1884   *History of Rockland County, New York.* J.B. Beers &
         Co., New York.

Colony, R.J.
1923   *The Magnetite Iron Deposits of Southeastern New York.* New York State Museum Bulletin Nos. 249-250. Albany, The University of the State of New York.

Davis, F.A., and H.L. Kochersperger
1876   "Map of Haverstraw Township." In *Combination Atlas of Rockland County, New York.* F.A. Davis & Co., Philadelphia.

Defense Plant Corporation
1943   *Peters Mine General Plan.* Alan Wood Steel Co., Ringwood, New Jersey. Map on file, North Jersey Highlands Historical Society Library, Ringwood, New Jersey.

Dupont, Ronald J., Jr.
1992   *Vernon 200: A Bicentennial History of the Township of Vernon, New Jersey.* The Friends of the Dorothy E. Henry Library, McAfee, New Jersey.

Federal Writers' Project.
1939   *The WPA Guide to 1930s New Jersey.* Reprinted in 1986 by Rutgers University Press, New Brunswick, New Jersey.

French. F.F., W.F. Wood and S.N. Beers
1859   *Map of Orange and Rockland Counties.* Corey & Backman, Publisher, Philadelphia.

Geological Survey of New Jersey
1881   *Annual Report of the State Geologist.* Trenton, N.J.: John L. Murphy, Printer.

Green, Frank Bertangue, M.D.
1886   *The History of Rockland County.* A.S. Barnest Co., New York.

Hardesty, Donald L.
1988   *The Archaeology of Mining and Miners: A View from The Silver State.* Special Publications Series No. 6, The Society for Historical Archaeology. Printed by Braun-Brumfield, Ann Arbor, Michigan.

Haugland, Gary
1993   "Thomas A. Edison: Absentee Landowner in Doodletown." *Trailside Museum & Zoo Historical Papers,* Number H-3, pp. 1-6. Palisades Interstate Park, Bear Mountain, New York.

Hewitt, Edward Ringwood
1947   *Ringwood Manor, The Home of the Hewitts.* Second Printing. Trenton, N.J.: Trenton Printing Co. Inc.

Hoeferlin, William
1955   *Hikers Region Map No. 5, Northern Ramapo Mountains.* Brooklyn, New York.

1964   *Hikers Region Map No. 13, Pompton Hills-Butler, New Jersey.* Brooklyn, New York.

1964   *Hikers Region Map No. 18, Harriman Park Northern Area.* Brooklyn, New York.

1964   *Hikers Region Map No. 36, Wuwayanda Plateau, New Jersey.* Brooklyn, New York.

1965   *Hikers Region Map No. 5, Northern Ramapo Mountains.* Brooklyn, New York.

1965   *Hikers Region Map No. 21, Greenwood Lake, NY-NJ.* Brooklyn, New York.

1966   *Harriman Park Trail Guide.* Walking News, Brooklyn, New York.

Kitchell, William
1856   *Second Annual Report on the Geological Survey of the State of New Jersey, For the Year 1855.* New Jersey Geological Survey, Trenton.

Kummel, Henry B. and C.C. Vermeule
1901   *A Geological Map of the Green Pond Mountain Region in Morris and Passaic Counties.* Geological Survey of New Jersey, Trenton, New Jersey.

Lenik, Edward J., JoAnn Cotz and Kathleen L. Ehrhardt
1984   *Cultural Resource Survey of the Monksville Reservoir Project Area, Passaic County, New Jersey.* Sheffield Archaeological Consultants, Wayne, New Jersey.

Lenik, Edward J. and Kathleen L. Ehrhardt
1986   Data Recovery Excavations in the Monksville *Reservoir Project Area, Passaic County, New Jersey.* Volume I. Sheffield Archaeological Consultants, Wayne, New Jersey.

Lenik, Edward J., Ronald J. Dupont, Jr., and Thomas P. Fitzpatrick.
1989   *State 1A and 1B Cultural Resources Investigation of the Diamond Valley Farms Subdivision Property, Town of Ramapo, Rockland County, New York.* Sheffield Archaeological Consultants, Wayne, New Jersey

Lenik, Edward J. and Diane Dallal
1990   *Cultural Resources Investigation of the Sterling Forest Tract, Borough of Ringwood and Township of West Milford, Passaic County, New Jersey.* Sheffield Archaeological Consultants, Butler, New Jersey.

Lewis, Warren D.
1968   "Wawayanda State Park." In *Forest and Park Notes #2.* Trenton, New Jersey.

Munsell, W.W.
1882   *History of Morris County, New Jersey.* W.W. Munsell & Co., New York.

Myles, William J.
1992   *Harriman Trails. A Guide and History.* New York-New Jersey Trail Conference, Inc., New York.

New York-New Jersey Trail Conference, Inc.
1984   *New York Walk Book.* 5th Edition. Anchor Press, Doubleday, New York.

1995   *Trail Map 3, Harriman Park-South Half.* New York, New York.

1995   *Trail Map 4, Harriman Park-North Half.* New York, New York.

1991   *Pyramid Mountain Trails, Boonton-Montville, New Jersey.* New York, New York.

O'Connor, R.F.
1854   *Map of Rockland County, New York.* R.F. O'Connor, Publisher, New York.

Orange County Historical Society
        Archival records. On file, Arden, New York.

Peele, Robert, Editor
1941   *Mining Engineers Handbook.* 3rd Edition. Wiley, New York.

Poyneer, Norma Charleston
1992   "A Reminiscence: My Grandfather and Father." *Trailside Museum & Zoo Historical Papers*, Number H-17, p. 1. Palisades Interstate Park, Bear Mountain, New York.

Pustay, M.R. and T.K. Shea
1982   *Abandoned Iron Mines of Sussex County, New Jersey.*
        New Jersey Department of Labor, Division of Work
        Place Standards, Office of Safety Compliance,
        Trenton, New Jersey.

1992   *Abandoned Iron Mines of Kinnelon, Boonton,
        Montville & Riverdale Townships, Morris County, New
        Jersey.* New Jersey Department of Labor, Division of
        Work Place Standards, Office of Safety Compliance,
        Trenton, New Jersey.

Ransom, James M.
1966   *Vanishing Ironworks of the Ramapos.* Rutgers
        University Press, New Brunswick, New Jersey.

Roome, Benjamin & Sons
1874-76 *Maps and Descriptions of Lands Lying in the Town-
        ship of Pompton and West Milford, Passaic County,
        N.J., Belonging to Messrs. Edward Cooper and Abram
        S. Hewitt, Also of the Lands Adjoining as Surveyed
        and Mapped.* On file, North Jersey Highlands
        Historical Society Library, Ringwood, New Jersey.

Rosa, C. Boehm
1938   "Green Recalls Boyhood Work in O'Neill Shaft." A
        four-part series entitled "Mining: An Orange County
        Industry for Two Centuries." Unpaged, 7 May.
        Middletown Times-Herald, Middletown, New York.
        Copy on file, Newburgh Free Library, Newburgh, New
        York.

Salisbury, R.D.
1894   *Preliminary Map of the Surface Formation of the
        Valley of the Passaic.* Geological Survey of New
        Jersey, Trenton, New Jersey.

Sessions, Ralph
1985   *Woodsmen, Mountaineers and Bockies: The People of the Ramapos.* The Historical Society of Rockland County, New City, New York.

Stevenot, M. Smeltzer
1992   "The Charlestons of St. Johns." *Trailside Museum & Zoo Historical Papers.* Number H-8, p. 2. Palisades Interstate Park, Bear Mountain, New York.

Sidney, J.C.
1851   *Map of Orange County, New York.* Newell S. Brown, Publisher, Newburgh, New York.

Tholl, Claire K.
1970   *The Mines of Ringwood* (booklet). The North Jersey Highlands Historical Society, Newfoundland, New Jersey.

Tompkins, Arthur S., Editor
1902   *Historical Record of Rockland County, New York.* Van Deusen & Joyce, Nyack, New York.

Vermeule, C.C.
1884   "A Topographic Map of the Northeastern Highlands." Atlas Sheet No. 4. In *Atlas of New Jersey.* Geological Survey of New Jersey. Julius Bien & Co., New York.

1884   "A Topographic Map of the Counties of Bergen, Hudson, and Essex." Atlas Sheet No. 7. In *Atlas of New Jersey.* Geological Survey of New Jersey. Julius Bien & Co., New York.

Walking News Inc.
1983   *Hikers Region Map No. 16, Harriman Park E.-Bear Mountain.* New York, New York.

Young, George J.
1923   *Elements of Mining.* Second Edition. McGraw-Hill Book Co., Inc., New York.

Index